Twayne's English Authors Series

EDITOR OF THIS VOLUME

Sylvia E. Bowman

Indiana University

Richard Aldington

TEAS 222

Richard Aldington

RICHARD ALDINGTON

By RICHARD EUGENE SMITH

Lamar University

TWAYNE PUBLISHERS
A DIVISION OF G. K. HALL & CO., BOSTON

Library of Congress Cataloging in Publication Data

Smith, Richard Eugene.
  Richard Aldington.

  (Twayne's English authors series ; TEAS 222)
  Bibliography: p. 191–96
  Includes index.
  1. Aldington, Richard, 1892–1962—Criticism and
interpretation.
PR6001.L4Z79   821'.9'12   77-24042
ISBN 0-8057-6691-X

Contents

About the Author

Richard Eugene Smith received his M.A. from the University of Michigan and his B.A. and Ph.D. from the University of Utah. He has taught at the University of Utah and at Weber State College. Before joining the Department of English at Lamar University, where he is currently teaching, he was employed as a faculty member of the Extension Class Division of Utah State University. In addition to English composition and surveys of literature, he has taught courses in mythology, creative writing, the short story, and the British novel. He is a member of the Modern Language Association of America and of the Rocky Mountain Modern Language Association.

Dr. Smith's specialty is twentieth-century British literature. He is at present working on a study of the novels of Wilfrid Sheed. Another of his major interests is the influence of the Japanese upon modern British and American literature, an interest acquired as a graduate student at the Center for Japanese Studies at the University of Michigan. A result of this interest has been his published criticism of Ezra Pound and the *haiku*. An amateur actor himself, Dr. Smith is also preparing a study of the influence of the *Noh* drama upon the plays of W. B. Yeats.

Preface

Richard Aldington is best known as one of the leaders of the imagist movement during the second decade of the twentieth century. His role as an imagist poet and theorist, however, was only a small part of a literary career which lasted nearly fifty years and which witnessed the publication of more than a hundred different books in England and in America. He continued to write poetry for many years after imagism had ceased to function as a movement, and his volumes include a series of long poems which embody a variety of poetic techniques. In addition, he has produced several novels and collections of short stories, the majority of which have been republished in other languages. He has also published many biographies, translations, and volumes of critical essays; and he has edited and written introductions to a large number of books.

In spite of his achievements, Aldington has remained a comparatively little known author; and scholarly treatment of his life and works has been sketchy and inadequate. This neglect may be attributed largely to the reception of his highly controversial (but very well-documented) biography of Lawrence of Arabia. Not only was it one of his last books, but it apparently colored the views of many critics toward his earlier literary accomplishments, with unfortunate results.

The aim of the present study is to present a more comprehensive survey of Aldington's writings than has hitherto been attempted, and to begin with an account of his life and character. The first chapter shows that Aldington was essentially a man with a positive attitude toward life—a man with a love for life, travel, natural beauty, literature and the arts—and this attitude is reflected in his writings. Though not a major writer himself, he was closely associated with some of the greatest British and American writers of the twentieth century, among them Ezra Pound, T. S. Eliot, and D. H. Lawrence. Aldington's personal acquaintance with D. H. Lawrence is evident in his biography, *Portrait of a Genius But. . . .*

The account of Aldington's life is followed by a critical analysis of his poetry and prose fiction, but only brief mention is made of his less creative writings. In addition to the imagist poems and his famous war novel, *Death of a Hero,* his best long poems are *Life Quest, The Crystal World,* and *A Fool i' the Forest.* His other good novels are *All Men Are Enemies, The Colonel's Daughter, Seven Against Reeves,* and *The Romance of Casanova.* Along with *Death of a Hero,* all but the last of these novels are satires on English society. Two collections of short stories, *Roads to Glory* and *Soft Answers,* must also be included among his best prose fiction. The latter is of special interest to the student of literature, for it contains lampoons on famous writers whom the author had known, the most important of whom are Ezra Pound and T. S. Eliot.

The study concludes with a summary of the author's work and with an evaluation of his contribution to literature. It points out that, despite their faults, his writings are characterized by "vigor," "integrity," and "individualism." It also adds that Aldington was a very versatile and talented man of letters who produced important work in several different genres of literature. Finally, it indicates that his best poetry and prose fiction should survive as "minor classics" of the twentieth century.

RICHARD E. SMITH

Lamar University

Acknowledgments

I express my gratitude to those who have given me assistance in preparing this study of Richard Aldington. I am most grateful to Professors Jack Garlington (who first suggested the study), Thomas J. Sobchack, and John Vernon of the University of Utah English Department for invaluable criticism of my manuscript; to Maude J. Richards, Walker S. Lane, Annie Laurie Bearry, and other staff members of the Weber State College and University of Utah Libraries for helping me locate and obtain materials for my study; to Dr. Sylvia E. Bowman and Alberta M. Hines for their patience and understanding with respect to the problems which I encountered in writing the book; to my wife, my children, and my parents for their support and encouragement. I also thank Allan Wingate (Publishers) Ltd. for permission to quote from *The Complete Poems of Richard Aldington*, copyright 1948.

Chronology

1892   Richard Aldington (christened Edward Godfree Aldington) born July 8 at Portsmouth, England, the son of a middle-class lawyer.

1907   Begins to take a serious interest in poetry.

1910   Enrolls in University College, London.

1911   Loss of family fortune makes it necessary for Aldington to leave London University and seek employment as a writer.

1912   Meets Brigit Patmore, Ezra Pound, H. D. (Hilda Doolittle), Harold Monro, William Butler Yeats, and other people of importance in the literary world. Imagist movement founded by Pound, H. D., and Aldington. November, Aldington publishes first imagist poems in *Poetry* (Chicago).

1913   Travels in Italy. October, marries H. D.

1914   Becomes literary editor of *The Egoist*. Contributes poems to first imagist anthology, *Des Imagistes*. Meets D. H. Lawrence.

1915   Publishes poems in second imagist anthology, *Some Imagist Poets*, and in his first book, *Images (1910–1915)*. Publishes his first translations.

1916–   Enlists in British army as a private and rises to rank of cap-
1918   tain. Contributes poems to the 1916 and 1917 imagist anthologies, *Some Imagist Poets*. Publishes *Myrrhine and Konallis* (poems) and some translations. Meets T. S. Eliot.

1919   Returns to London upon discharge from army. Separates from H. D.; lives with Dorothy Yorke. Begins work as critic of French literature for the London *Times Literary Supplement*. *Images of War* and *Images of Desire* (books of poems).

1921   *Medallions in Clay*, a volume of translations.

1923   *Exile and Other Poems*. Publishes some translations.

1924   *A Fool i' the Forest*, a long poem. *Literary Studies and Reviews*, a book of critical essays. Several volumes of translations.

1925   *Voltaire*, a study of the life and works.

1926   *French Studies and Reviews*, a collection of critical essays.

1927   Publishes a number of translations.

1928   Begins living and traveling with Brigit Patmore. Two new translations.

1929   *Death of a Hero*, a novel. *The Eaten Heart*, a long poem. *Remy de Gourmont*, translations of selections from the works.

1930   *Roads to Glory*, a book of short stories. *A Dream in the Luxembourg*, a long poem. Publishes some important new translations. Meets Norman Douglas.

1931   *The Colonel's Daughter*, a novel.

1932   *Soft Answers*, a volume of short stories.

1933   *All Men Are Enemies*, a novel.

1934   *Women Must Work*, a novel.

1935   First visit to the United States. *Life Quest*, a long poem. *Artifex*, a collection of essays.

1937   *Very Heaven*, a novel. *The Crystal World*, a long poem.

1938   *Seven Against Reeves*, a novel. Divorces H. D.; breaks off with Brigit Patmore; marries Netta McCulloch. Daughter Catherine born eighteen months later. Establishes residence in the United States.

1939   *Rejected Guest*, a novel.

1941   *Life for Life's Sake*, an autobiography. Edits *The Viking Book of Poetry of the English-Speaking World*, an anthology.

1943   *The Duke*, a biography of the duke of Wellington.

1944   Moves to Los Angeles, California, where he is employed as a Hollywood script writer.

1946   *The Romance of Casanova*, a novel. Returns to France; establishes permanent residence there.

1947   Receives the James Tait Black Memorial Prize for his biography of the duke of Wellington.

1948   *The Complete Poems of Richard Aldington*. *Four English Portraits*, a volume of biographical sketches.

1949   *The Strange Life of Charles Waterton*, a biography.

1950   *D. H. Lawrence, Portrait of a Genuis But . . .* , a biography. Separates from his wife, Netta.

1954   *Pinorman*, a book of reminiscences.

1955   *Lawrence of Arabia*, a biography first published in France in 1954.

1956   *Introduction to Mistral*, a study of the life and works of the Provençal poet.

1957   *Frauds,* a book of essays and biographical sketches. *Portrait of a Rebel: The Life and Works of Robert Louis Stevenson.*
1959   Receives the Prix de Gratitude Mistralienne for his *Introduction to Mistral.*
1962   Accepts invitation from Soviet Writers' Union to visit Russia. Celebrates seventieth birthday in Moscow. Becomes ill shortly after his return to France and dies on July 27 at his cottage near the village of Sury-en-Vaux.

CHAPTER 1

The Man

I *Childhood*

RICHARD Aldington (christened Edward Godfree Aldington) was born at Portsmouth, England, on July 8, 1892, the son of a middle-class lawyer. While he was still very young, his family moved to Dover and lived for a time on the High Street amid the busy bustle of crowds and horses. In Aldington's autobiography,[1] the primary source of information about the first thirty-eight years of his life, he tells of missing the trees, the flowers, and the wheat fields of his former home; and when the family changed its residence to a yellow brick house surrounded by trees and gardens, he regarded the move as advantageous. At the same time, he was sent to a private school to begin his studies in French and Latin, but was often late for class because he was unable to resist the temptation to linger about the greenhouses of the next-door florist. This early love of nature is reflected in the vivid scenic descriptions which became an important characteristic of his writing.

It was therefore fortunate that, before he was ten, he began to spend his summers in the country where the Aldingtons soon established residence; but he continued to remain at school in Dover for the greater part of the year. He calls the relatively brief periods on the "bleak, nearly treeless upland of chalk down" of the South Foreland as "the more important" of his life, while explaining that "in the town I was being manufactured into the sort of human product a not too intelligent provincial society thought I should be; whereas, in the country, I was busily but unconsciously developing into something on my own" (*LL* 17–18). In spite of the fierce winter storms and the concomitant spectacles of frequent shipwrecks and rescues that Aldington witnessed, he remembers best the pleasant summers when he amused himself by climbing the dangerous cliffs, collecting

15

butterflies among the wild flowers, searching for creatures in pools left by the sea at low tide, fishing for prawns along the shore, and bicycling over the inland roads through a country "drenched in history" (LL, 24).

As a boy, Aldington also yearned to travel beyond Dover and its environs. One memorable experience of his childhood was a summer's day when he accompanied his parents across the Channel to Calais, which in clear weather he had often seen through his telescope. So delighted was he with the colorful little town and its relaxed and cheerful atmosphere that he resolved to visit France again. Eventually, he spent some of the best—as well as some of the worst—years of his life there; and France was his last home. He very nearly met a violent death there on the battlefield as a young man, and he finally died there of natural causes. For a time, however, he consoled himself by traveling about England during his summer vacations. During his adolescent years he began touring England on foot with an older friend and spent a fortnight walking across West England in 1910. Although he felt a lifelong contempt for most sports, hiking continued to be one of the few athletic activities which gave him great pleasure. In the meantime he also visited Antwerp and Brussels with his father. Since his first trip to Calais, he had found on the prewar Continent something more congenial with his own temperament than he had found in England.

At first, young Aldington's reading habits appear to have been random and undisciplined. As he grew older, he began to develop a genuine interest in literature and was fortunate to have a good library in his home. During the summer of his fifteenth year, he overheard some comments about a new set of Oscar Wilde's works which his father had just acquired. His curiosity was aroused, and, one day in the library, he picked up a volume that his father had left open, read a paragraph about Keats, and was entranced. Thanks to the completeness of his father's library, moreover, young Aldington had at his fingertips all the major English poets and many minor poets. He had covered them all within two years, a task made possible by an unspecified operation which left him free to do nothing but read for nearly a year. Upon entering University College, London, he discovered that he "had read every poet in the required English course, and scored about 98 out of 100 in a special test paper" given to him "by an incredulous faculty" (LL, 42).

His attempts to write poetry were almost simultaneous with his interest in reading it. The most influential of his acquaintances was a middle-aged neighbor who befriended him and became his "poetic guardian" during these early formative years; the latter read and criticized the boy's work regularly and gave him "whole-hearted encouragement" (*LL*, 50–51). Furthermore, the neighbor gave the sixteen-year-old an appreciation of the classics and an introduction to French and Italian poetry; and, as a result, the lad soon taught himself to read French fluently. There can be no doubt that this moment was a decisive one in determining the course of Aldington's adult career as a critic of French literature and as a translator of masterpieces from several European languages, both ancient and modern.

Before he was seventeen, Aldington had one of his poems published in a London magazine; but, owing to a cultivated neighbor's disapproval, he delayed submitting any more of his work. Furthermore, his mother had just humiliated him by sending his first short story, a piece that he had read in private to her and an aunt, to George Bernard Shaw, who had acknowledged it with cynical good humor and a guinea. The boy never discovered his mother's motive, but he was probably right in suspecting that she had hoped that Shaw would "turn his satire on me and drastically cure me of the itch for writing" (*LL*, 59–60). In later years, Aldington told a friend that his mother was "a strong, self-willed woman who had dominated both a gentle husband and a gentle son."[2] A writer herself, she had published at least one successful, if ephemeral, book, *Love-letters That Never Reached Him*, which her son had disliked intensely.[3] Apparently she was opposed to the boy's ambition to become a poet; she preferred instead that he pursue an ordinary profession; therefore, his enrollment in University College, London, in 1910, after "three or four lifeless months at Harrow" (*LL*, 63–64), seems to have been in defiance of his mother's wish that he follow in his father's footsteps and become a lawyer.[4]

II *Preparation for a Literary Career*

Aldington was much happier at the university than he had been at the public schools of Dover and Harrow. Moreover, he enjoyed his contacts with some of his fellow students such as Alec Randall, who later joined the diplomatic service, received a knighthood, and remained a friend. To Randall, "Richard became the centre of a group of admiring friends . . . with his handsome features, his sparkling

merry eyes, his reddish beard and velvet jacket and flowing bow
tie":

> He was also a rebel. . . . His defiance of authority, which was gay and far
> from angry, his enthusiasm for modern French poetry—all this delighted
> us, and communicated itself to us. . . . As for politics Richard was a
> thorough individualist, and remained so all his life. He preferred the "pure
> art" of Wilde and Yeats to Shaw's political social tracts dressed up as drama.
> He could not share our enthusiasm for the social reform ideas of Mr. and
> Mrs. Sidney Webb. . . . Richard was by no means a snob, but there was
> about him then a trace of the Horatian "odi profanum vulgus et arceo." As
> he grew older the manipulation of the masses by politicians through a highly
> centralized government became more and more antipathetic to him.[5]

These recollections of Aldington as a merry young man are especially worth noting, since other persons who knew him less well and
who admired him less have apparently created the myth that he was
an angry and embittered man throughout his life. Randall too seems
to have been troubled by the element of "bitterness" which he must
have discovered later in a few of Aldington's publications, but he
was never aware of this element in the personality of the man himself.[6] In Randall's final comment about the friendship which continued until Aldington's death, he says that "The picture of Richard
that will always be in my mind is that of a merry, humorous, kindly
man."[7]

Randall also mentions Aldington's aversion to politics and to ideas
of social reform. As Aldington himself states, he had early "begun to
suspect the ability of revolutionary idealists to make good their
glittering promises or even to maintain the status quo of comparative well-being they overthrew, or wished to overthrow, as unjust
and oppressive." To this statement he adds "another reason for
avoiding any active part in politics," either as a liberal or a conservative; to him, "the great mass of the community is supposed to worry
and to feel responsible without any more power than casting an
occasional vote which will very likely not have the slightest
influence anyway" (LL, 93). Organized religion was just as distaste-
ful to him, for he believed that politics, social reform, and religion
were all futile enterprises dominated by hypocrisy and cant. Lacking faith in the combined efforts of men to create a genuinely better
life for themselves, he set forth on a long quest for personal happi-

ness and fulfillment—hoping, of course, that a few others might follow his example.

An unexpected increase in his parents' income had been responsible for Aldington's opportunity to attend the university. In 1911, when his father lost a great deal of money through "a complicated series of speculations," the son was obliged to leave the university and find a job *(LL, 78)*. Rather than accept a position as a clerk in a big London company, with a salary starting at forty pounds annually and with an eventual chance to earn five hundred, he chose to accept part-time employment as an assistant to the sports editor of a London newspaper, despite the positive hatred which he had felt toward organized sports since his public-school days. In exchange for reporting two or three events a week, he received the regular commission for the stories, plus the fringe benefit of sharing the Bloomsbury flat of his employer who also provided him with letters of introduction to editors of other London periodicals that would occasionally buy his poems. At the end of the first week, he discovered that reporting sports and writing poetry had earned him as much as he would have obtained for an entire month of full-time work as a clerk in an office.

Although Aldington was not so naive as to believe that he would be this fortunate every week, he decided to cast his chances with the more precarious, but more attractive, mode of supporting himself: "What interested me was a way of life, the way of life of a good European. I wanted to know and to enjoy the best that had been thought and felt and known through the ages—architecture, painting, sculpture, poetry, literature, food and wine, France and Italy, women, old towns, beautiful country" *(LL* 85–86). From this time on, Aldington tried to express his concept of a "good European" in both his own life and in his writings.

For a few months after leaving the university, Aldington led a lonely but not unhappy life; he presumably spent most of his time reading and writing, though he often visited art galleries and sometimes theaters and music halls. It was not long, however, before he had made friends among other important young poets, Harold Monro and two American expatriates, Ezra Pound and H. D. (Hilda Doolittle). Through Pound and Monro, he rapidly became acquainted with many other people associated with the literary world, but he found most of their formal parties and dinners "tedious and intolerable," for "There was a pretentiousness about such people which I couldn't stand." On the other hand, he enjoyed the social gatherings at Yeats' lodgings in Woburn Place, even though he, like Hotspur with Glendower in *Henry IV*, "grew a little weary of spooks, fairies, elementals, sorcerers" *(LL*, 106–7). About this time, he also met May Sinclair, Sturge Moore, the Italian poet Marinetti, and probably Lady Augusta Gregory and George Moore. In cultivating friendship with Pound and H. D., moreover, Aldington alienated himself from a group of his own countrymen who were later known as the Georgian poets; but he did not regret such alienation since he felt that these writers were "regional in their outlook and in love with littleness." Pound's cosmopolitanism and H. D.'s aesthetic "genius" were much more to his liking *(LL*, 110–11).

Spring, 1912, found Aldington in Paris with no definite plans as to when he would return to England. Indeed, he appeared to be abandoning a career which had been steadily improving in London. In addition to the regular sales of poems and sports articles with which he had begun, he had had a couple of other articles published in the newspapers and was writing reviews for the *Poetry Review*, a new periodical which was edited by his friend Harold Monro. Furthermore, he was continuing to form an increasing number of literary acquaintances in London. A move to the Continent might have been unfeasible, however, if his parents had not provided him with a modest amount of money for expenses each month, since his pleasure trip bore no prospect of any financial return. He "fell in love with Paris at first sight" *(LL*, 115), and, spent most of his time sight-seeing and enjoying life, often in the company of Pound and H. D.

After a brief sojourn in Paris, Aldington returned to his work in London; but the following winter—depressed by the weather and encouraged by a postcard from Genoa, by forty dollars from *Poetry* magazine in Chicago for three poems, by his monthly allowance from his parents, and by a commission from the *New Age* to write some articles on life abroad—he departed for Italy, expecting to be there a maximum of two months but staying almost seven. He spent the first eight weeks in Rome; the remainder of the time in Capri, Naples, Florence, and Venice; but he also visited Amalfi, Cava, Paestum, Pompeii, and Sorrento in the south, and Padua, Verona, Vicenza, and Lake Garda in the north. Violet Hunt had provided him with letters of introduction to Violet Gibson and R. B.

Cunninghame Graham. Mrs. Gibson helped him find lodgings in Rome and conducted him on sight-seeing trips to points of interest unspoiled by tourism, while Graham helped him become acquainted with the Roman nobility. In addition, Aldington met Alice Meynell, who was a disappointment to him even though he had liked her poetry, and Stefan George, who fascinated him with conversation about Verlaine, Mallarmé, and other symbolist poets with whom George had been friends.

III   *The Imagist*

Aldington's three poems in the November, 1912, issue of Harriet Monroe's newly founded *Poetry* had much more significance than merely providing him with an incentive to see Italy. They were the first published poems to be identified with the imagist movement, which was founded in a Kensington tea shop by Aldington, H. D., and Pound. Pound instigated the founding, adopted the term, provided the initial leadership, and negotiated with Harriet Monroe for the privilege of using her magazine as an organ to publish the poems and to promote the poetic theories of the group.[8] A statement was also included in the second issue of *Poetry* that classified Aldington as "one of the 'Imagistes,' a group of ardent Hellenists . . . pursuing interesting experiments in *vers libre;* trying to attain in English certain subtleties of cadence of the kind which Mallarmé and his followers . . . studied in French."[9] Thus, in November, 1912, Richard Aldington had the honor at the age of twenty of being the first (and youngest) official imagist.

The imagists, however, needed a periodical of their own. Two London feminists, Dora Marsden and Harriet Shaw Weaver, had begun fortnightly publication of *The New Freewoman: An Individualist Review* in June, 1913; and Pound managed to persuade them that they should have a section devoted to contemporary literature. Imagist poems began to appear in the paper in September, and the name of the publication was advantageously changed to *The Egoist: An Individualist Review* on the first of January of the following year. The publishers agreed that the imagists were to have complete control over the content of each issue, with the exception of the "leading article." At the outset, Aldington became "assistant editor" (the literary editor) of *The Egoist*, a title which he shared with H. D. in 1916 when he joined the army. A year later, in 1917, T. S. Eliot replaced them both as assistant editor, and retained the post until the paper was discontinued in 1919.[10]

At approximately the same time that Pound was helping found *The Egoist*, he began to compile the first imagist anthology; for he was especially interested in attracting attention to the verse of H. D. and Aldington. Since these poets' combined productions were too meager for a book, he chose seven pieces by H. D. and ten by Aldington as a "nucleus" and gathered contributions from other members of the movement, including Skipwith Cannell, John Cournos, F. S. Flint, Ford Madox Ford, James Joyce, Amy Lowell, Allen Upward, William Carlos Williams, and himself. The book, published early in 1914, was entitled *Des Imagistes: An Anthology*.

Although Pound soon deserted the cause, his doing so did not prevent the other imagists from continuing the movement. In 1915, 1916, and 1917 they published three anthologies, each with the title of *Some Imagist Poets*, under the chairmanship of Amy Lowell. The contributors to the volumes were always the same six poets. England was represented by Richard Aldington, F. S. Flint, and D. H. Lawrence; America, by H. D., John Gould Fletcher, and Amy Lowell; and these representatives made the movement a truly Anglo-American enterprise. These three anthologies not only established imagism as an important movement but also aroused interest and criticism in both England and America. Although the criticism was largely unfavorable, the series sold very well,[11] especially in America where the imagists were soon recognized for their achievement and where later anthologies have often included selections from the first ones.[12]

The imagists themselves, however, did not attempt to publish another anthology until 1929—they had accomplished their purpose of bringing widespread attention to the movement, and American intervention in World War I added to their difficulties. In 1929, Aldington, in an effort to prove that imagism was not dead, gathered contributions from most of the poets who had been involved in the movement and published the *Imagist Anthology, 1930*.[13] Ten years later, he asked and answered the question, "What did the Imagists achieve between 1912 and 1917?":

Well, they did some useful pioneering work. They dealt a blow at the post-Victorian magazine poets, whose unappeased shades still clamour for Imagist blood. They livened things up a lot. They made free verse popular—it had already been used by Blake, Whitman, and Henley and by many of the French Symbolistes. And they tried to attain an exacting if narrow standard of style in poetry. And to a considerable extent T. S. Eliot and his followers have carried on their operations from positions won by the Imagists. (*LL*, 133)

Aldington also denied that he was "the Fuehrer of the Imagists"; to him, "The fame or otherwise of Ducedom must go to Ezra [Pound], who invented the 'movement' . . . and to Amy Lowell, who put it across" (*LL*, 133).

When Aldington and H. D. were married in October, 1913, she was nearly six years older than her husband; he was twenty-one in July, and she had just turned twenty-seven on September 10. Information about their marriage may be gleaned from H. D.'s novel, *Bid Me to Live*, which she wrote after World War II but did not publish until 1960. In an interview, she frankly admitted that the novel was entirely autobiographical: "It's just that, word for word. It is a *roman à clef*, and the keys are easy enough to find. . . . I am Julia. And all the others are real people."[14]

If H. D. is the Julia of the novel, it is obvious that Aldington is Rafe, the husband; and it is quite safe to suppose that the book contains a true account of the real marriage, qualified only by the writer's art, memory, and point of view. To some extent, a comparison of various details in *Bid Me to Live* and *Death of a Hero*, Aldington's own autobiographical novel, may cast additional light on the truth, although Aldington's book is certainly a mixture of fact and fiction. Moreover, the scarcity of information about Aldington's life is not difficult to explain when one examines the comments of some of his friends, such as Henry Williamson, who says that "Aldington was a shy man . . . but . . . he was more guarded than shy. He was hospitable and kind, in a remote way; he had been hurt in his early years, one saw that much in his writings."[15] Sir Alec Randall, who had known him since they were both students at University College, London, remarks, "He did not confide in me any of his domestic troubles."[16] A younger friend, Lawrence Durrell, complains that "he never spoke about his private life, his marriages, his personal affairs; indeed to this day I do not know anything about him as a human being, only as a writer."[17]

At any rate, in his autobiography Aldington remained silent about his courtship of H. D., their marriage, their honeymoon, and their life together. His only acknowledgment of the marriage may be found in a very brief reference to their daily habit during the summer following their marriage when they went together to the South Kensington Art Museum where they "sat in a large cool room overlooking a courtyard with a large fountain" and "read books on Italy and Italian art" (*LL*, 161). They had planned to visit Italy later in the year, but approaching war compelled them to change their minds. The remainder of Aldington's account of the period between his debut into literary circles as a promising young poet and his enlistment in the British army as an ordinary "Tommy" is filled largely with anecdotes and discussions of other writers whom he knew, particularly Pound, Yeats, Amy Lowell, D. H. Lawrence, Ford Madox Ford, and Violet Hunt (who married Ford).

IV   *The War Years*

England entered the war on August 4, 1914. The following day, Aldington (on the advice of T. E. Hulme, who defended militarism on philosophical grounds)[18] attempted to volunteer for the army, but was rejected because of his operation four years earlier. Despite his willingness to fight for his country, he was not really enthusiastic about taking an active part in the hostilities as either a soldier or a propagandist. He asserts that he "had lost the romantic-heroic idea of war" during his university days by reading about Walt Whitman's Civil War experiences, which had motivated him to work for a time for the Garton Peace Foundation upon his return from Paris in 1912 (*LL*, 119–20). Soon after the war began, he accepted part-time employment as secretary to Ford Madox Ford, at the time that the latter was working for C. F. G. Masterman, the British minister of education, on a propaganda book against Germany, *When Blood is Their Argument.* [19] When the book was completed, Aldington helped Ford with the research on another work of propaganda for Masterman, *Between St. Dennis and St. George;* but he says, "I got so fed up with Ford I quit, and Alec Randall took over, finished the second book (I had begun with F.) and got the job at the F. O. I should have had" (*LL*, 154–55).[20]

During 1914–1915 Aldington was busy. In 1915 he had his first collection of poetry, *Images (1910–1915)*, published by Monro's Poetry Bookshop (reprinted the following year in America as *Images Old and New*); and two of his translations, *The Poems of Anyte of Tegea* and *Latin Poems of the Renaissance*, were published by the

Egoist Press. He was also translating Remy de Gourmont's work for periodicals in England and America in an effort to help the old friend who had been impoverished by the war. The winter before Aldington enlisted in the army, he went with H. D. to northern Devonshire, where they joined two other writers, J. M. Whitham and Carl Fallas, acquaintances of their friend John Cournos who arrived later. This "idyllic existence," as Aldington calls it, lasted only a few months. Around June, 1916,[21] Aldington and Fallas enlisted together. Though Fallas looked forward to the combat as a great adventure, Aldington felt that it was "a high price to pay for gratifying one's curiosity" (*LL*, 177); but he also believed that "it was a plain duty to be in the army, and cowardly to be out of it," and that it was "ridiculous and presumptuous to set up one's little conscience against the conscience of a nation" (*LL*, 170–71).

At the induction center, Aldington was appalled by the unsanitary conditions. He was then sent to a training camp near Corfe Castle in Dorsetshire where he was dismayed by the "spit-and-polish soldiering" and by the lack of preparation for combat, which did not really begin until after the men had arrived at the front (*LL*, 178). At the end of the initial training period, Aldington and Fallas were promoted to lance corporals and given additional training as noncommissioned officers before they were sent to a camp near Calais. Soon afterwards, they were assigned to an engineer battalion, and Aldington became a "runner" for his unit:

> It would be tedious to enumerate at length all my lucky chances and escapes. . . . It was by chance that I was given just one night off . . . when a shell dropped on a group of our officers and runners. . . . It was by chance that I lowered my head just as a shell burst beside me in a mine crater. . . . It was by chance that . . . I turned my head to speak to the man behind me exactly at the moment a large chunk of shell whizzed so close to my cheek that I felt its harsh and horrid breath. It was by chance that . . . my field glasses shifted round over my stomach—when I went to use them I found they had been smashed and bent. And finally . . . it was by chance that I missed the worst phase of two of the worst battles of the war. (*LL*, 186–87)

By way of summarizing his experiences, Aldington adds, "In my opinion I was a very poor soldier. . . . Not only did I fail to get killed myself . . . but I am perfectly certain I didn't kill anyone, and I know I saved the lives of two wounded Germans" (*LL*, 187).

Aldington must have been a better soldier than he admits, for he was sent to officer's training camp, received a commission in the Royal Sussex Regiment,[22] and ultimately rose to the rank of captain. He was still at the front when the conflict came to an end, for he led his unit in pursuit of the retreating Germans. On the morning following the Armistice, he was granted an early leave; and this event was unlucky because he had to report back to his battalion only a couple of days before an order came from the war office that would have allowed him to stay in England. As a result, he had to spend another three months in a Belgian village before he was released. Since he was still suffering from a bad case of shell shock, the strain of this prolonged active duty was especially hard on him. Indeed, he continued to suffer from his war experiences for the next eight years.

During the war, Aldington's marriage with H. D. had steadily deteriorated, and they had separated when he finally returned to London in mid-February, 1919. According to H. D.'s account in *Bid Me to Live*, they had hoped to emulate Robert and Elizabeth Barrett Browning but had succeeded only in maintaining a "Punch and Judy" relationship.[23] Due to a miscarriage accompanied by illness in 1915,[24] she had feared another pregnancy and was an inadequate mate for an "over-sexed officer on leave,"[25] even though her husband's visits from the front were short and infrequent. He, on the other hand, was desperately anxious to make the most of his brief leaves knowing that each one might be his last; and he tried hard to forget the horrors which were always behind and before him. Later he admitted that "through my own folly and worse, I had got my personal life into a tragical mess, which . . . resulted in separation from H. D." (*LL*, 206–7).

His "folly" was an affair with Dorothy ("Arabella") Yorke, a vivacious young American art student his own age who resided in the same building at 44 Mecklenburgh Square where H. D. had an apartment while he was in France.[26] H. D.'s novel implies that she tolerated her husband's infidelity until the affair got out of hand and his mistress demanded that he choose between them, which made the situation unbearable for H. D. and induced her to go away for a while with a young composer whom she had met.[27] Toward the end of the war, H. D. became pregnant again; and, just before her daughter Perdita was born, early in 1919, she contracted double pneumonia, which left her in poor health for some time.[28] At any rate, Aldington seems to have regretted the loss of his wife, but he apparently remained on intimate terms with Dorothy for several years afterward, at least until the winter of 1928.[29]

Although the war had interrupted his work, Aldington had published two volumes of poetry, *Reverie: A Little Book of Poems for H. D.* (1917) and *The Love of Myrrhine and Konallis, and Other Prose Poems* (1917), as well as two translations, *The Little Demon* by Feodor Sologub (1916) and *The Garland of Months* by Folgore Da San Gemignano (1917); John Cournos served as cotranslator of *The Little Demon.*

V   *The Postwar Years*

In view of the difficulty faced by many ex-officers in obtaining employment, Aldington was extremely fortunate. Shortly after his return, he wrote an article about the demobilization of the British army and had it published in a large daily newspaper, which advertised his survival of the war and his presence in England. By request of the editors, he sold to the *English Review* some old poems that had been rejected by the same periodical in 1915; and he became a contributor to two other literary magazines, *To-Day* and the *Anglo-French Review.* The Egoist Press agreed to reprint his earlier translations and to publish his new one, *Greek Songs in the Manner of Anacreon;* Elkin Mathews published his *Images of War: A Book of Poems.* The same year also witnessed the publication of two other volumes of poems, *Images* and *War and Love (1915–1918).*

In spite of this success, Aldington says that he "found it hard to concentrate on literary work, whether reading or writing" (*LL,* 207); he felt that his "creative vein had practically dried up" (*LL,* 210). His literary output was largely "stuff in hand" which he had written in his spare time in the army, and he knew that he needed steady employment, no matter how unpleasant it might be. But here again he was lucky. The summer before the war ended, Winifred Ellerman (who later achieved fame as an historical novelist under the *nom de plume* of "Bryher") had written to him in France of her interest in imagist poetry. He had referred her at once to H. D., and the two women had soon become close friends.[30] When the war was over, he applied—at first without success—for a job with *The Times Literary Supplement* as "critic of French literature," a position which John Middleton Murry was resigning in order to become editor of the *Athenaeum.* Shortly after arrival in London, Aldington was invited to dinner at the Ellerman's. Winifred's father, Sir John

Ellerman, who was a multimillionaire and a large shareholder in
The Times, willingly gave his guest a letter of introduction to the
editor of the newspaper. Thus, only two months after his discharge
from the army, Aldington had obtained the position he desired, a
job which he was to hold for the next ten years, even after Ellerman
had disposed of his shares in *The Times*.

Aldington's good fortune was tempered for a long time by his
shattered nerves and by his difficulty in adjusting to postwar England, for he had trouble finding identity with either his literary
friends or his former comrades in the army. On paying a visit to
Pound, he discovered that his former friend "had become violently
hostile to England" as the result of his loss of popularity and that
"this attitude did not seem a very good basis for a renewal of our old
intimacy" (*LL*, 216). On the other hand, he established new friendships with T. S. Eliot and Herbert Read, whom he had only recently
met; and he became acquainted with Osbert and Sacheverell Sit-
well.

Aldington soon grew weary of what he calls the "shams" and
"affectations" of London literary society and began to long for a
house in the country where he could live and work in peace while
recovering from the effects of his war experiences (*LL*, 227–28). In
December, 1919, he retired to the Chapel Farm Cottage at Hermitage in Berkshire which D. H. Lawrence had just vacated;[31] but he
later moved to another cottage near Aldermaston. For about seven
years, he led a quiet life in the country, which was interrupted only
at brief intervals by trips to London and the Continent: "This period
of about 1920–28 is now known as the 'gay twenties,' and I am
supposed to have been one of the maddest and merriest of the
gay-makers, *un petit Byron de nos jours*. . . . But in fact those years
were for me a period of almost continuous work, during which I
read widely and, between my own writing and translation, turned
out about 200,000 words a year. My routine was as regular as that of
any office worker, and my hours longer" (*LL*, 243). Notwithstanding
this regimen of hard work, he found time to cultivate vegetables and
flowers in his garden, and to visit nearby places of literary and
historical interest (which he later described in more detail in his
novel, *The Colonel's Daughter*). During the summers he frequently
had visitors: "Among the people who came to see me, Eliot was
most responsive to the history, Lawrence to the natural beauty and
the flowers" (*LL*, 259–60).

This Berkshire period was a very productive one for Aldington. Besides his regular articles about French literature for *The Times Literary Supplement,* he wrote for the *Nation* and for T. S. Eliot's *Criterion,* which he also served as editor of for a while. He also published twenty-seven books, many of which were issued in both English and American editions. In addition, he says, "I read continuously in French, English, and Italian, and taught myself to read Old French of the *langue d'oïl* and of the *langue d'oc.* I also read a good deal in the classics." When his father died of heart failure (*LL,* 293) in 1921, his mother gave him many of her husband's books, which included an almost complete collection of sixteenth- and seventeenth-century English drama; and he "read practically everything from *Gorboduc* and *Gammer Gurton's Needle* to Congreve" (*LL,* 264–65).

During the early part of the residence in Berkshire, Aldington had, however, published only one book a year. These books, all translations, were *The Poems of Meleager of Gadara* (1920), *Medallions in Clay* (1921), and *The Good Humoured Ladies* by Carlo Goldoni (1922). *Medallions in Clay,* however, was not a new piece of work but a republication in a single volume of *Greek Songs, Latin Poems, Anyte of Tegea,* and *Meleager of Gadara.* Upon completing his translation of *Voyages to the Moon and the Sun* by Cyrano de Bergerac around August, 1922, Aldington had enough money to make a trip to Italy where he spent September and October—his first trip abroad since the war.

In 1923 Aldington published five books, almost double the number for the previous three years. In addition to his translations, *French Comedies of the XVIIIth Century* and Cyrano de Bergerac's *Voyages,* he had three new volumes of poetry: *The Berkshire Kennet, Exile and Other Poems,* and *Collected Poems (1915–1923).* An even more productive year, 1924, witnessed the publication of a long poem called *A Fool i' the Forest* and a collection of critical essays entitled *Literary Studies and Reviews,* as well as four more translations: *Sturly* by Pierre Custot, *Dangerous Acquaintances* by Choderlos de Laclos, *A Book of Characters,* and *The Mystery of the Nativity.* At about this time, Aldington suffered a brief attack of poor health from overwork after he had finished a biographical-critical work, *Voltaire* (the only book he published in 1925). He was stricken with an illness that he believed at first to be heart failure, but which was diagnosed by a specialist as "rapid nervous exhaustion."

The doctor prescribed "absolute rest and change"; but, since the patient had already spent a couple of weeks in bed without any signs of recovery, he set out and "walked twenty miles a day through the most mountainous part of Wales for three weeks" (*LL*, 293–94):

> This psychological disturbance, simulating a real illness, was a strong indication of inner discontents and disharmonies. . . . The bi-annual escape to the Continent merely underlined this condition, if I may judge by the extreme regret with which I returned. Above all I was irritated and oppressed by having to spend nearly all my time in England, where some curious incompatibility between me and most of the people I met exasperated me.
> The desire to get away permanently from England became an obsession. (*LL*, 295)

The day had not yet come when Aldington could establish permanent residence abroad. When it did, he remained resolute in his decision never to live in England again.

During the spring in 1926, he made another trip to Italy and visited the hill towns in Tuscany and Umbria. He returned to England soon enough to take part in the general strike, which lasted more than a week, and performed various duties in London for *The Times* in order to keep the newspaper in circulation. For Aldington, however, the most important event in 1926 was his reunion with the Lawrences, who had been in America (they had actually returned to Europe the previous autumn). Since he had seen them last in 1919 and had exchanged few letters with them, he invited D. H. and Frieda to stay a few days with him in August at his Berkshire cottage:[32]

> In private talks Lawrence and I agreed that so far as we were concerned something had gone wrong with England, our England, so that we felt like aliens in our own home. The only thing to do, Lawrence insisted, was to get out and stay out (*LL*, 303). . . . In the intervals between working hours I thought of him a good deal. His talk and personality, the many glimpses of his life, gave point and concentration to the vague rebellious tendencies . . . in myself. Lawrence made less money than I did, but he was a free man; whereas I had one leg chained to a library and the other to the London literary press. (*LL*, 306–7)

Aldington must still have been concerned about the effects on his health of too much work, for he published only two books in 1926: a translation of *The Fifteen Joys of Marriage*, a fifteenth-century piece attributed to Antoine De La Sale; and a collection of critical essays, *French Studies and Reviews*, which had already appeared separately in periodicals. In October he joined the Lawrences for a brief time at the Villa Mirenda, Scandicci, Florence, for the grape harvest;[33] and he also spent some of that winter in Rome.

In 1927 Aldington began to live in Paris for the greater part of the year, renting an apartment across from the Luxembourg garden, but he returned to England in the winter. That year he published five books, a record output since his breakdown from overwork. They included a small volume on D. H. Lawrence and several translations (*Candide and Other Romances* by Voltaire, *Letters of Voltaire and Madame du Deffand*, and *Letters of Madame de Sévigné*). To Aldington, 1928 was "a year of activity and change" (*LL*, 319), during which he realized an income of more than a thousand pounds and produced a few new books, among them a very brief study of Remy de Gourmont and two translations, *The Treason of the Intellectuals* by Julien Benda and *Fifty Romance Lyric Poems*. Spring found him in Paris again, where he continued to follow his habit of completing his day's work before socializing with other writers in the cafés; but he had much leisure time, for he found it unnecessary to spend more than half of each day at his writing. In the summer he returned to his cottage in Berkshire and assisted Lawrence in the illegal occupation of distributing *Lady Chatterley's Lover* to the subscribers; for, even though Aldington believed that it was not a first-rate novel, he was in favor of Lawrence's purpose in writing it.

While living in Paris, Aldington saw James Joyce occasionally, but the two men were never intimate. Among his American acquaintances in Paris were Ernest Hemingway, Hart Crane, and Thomas Wolfe. He also became friends with Jean Paulhan, who edited the *Nouvelle Revue Française;* and he was permitted to use Paulhan's retreat on the Île de Port-Cros on the French Riviera during October and November, 1928. In mid-October, the Lawrences joined him on the island,[34] but they remained only a month, since the weather was bad in November and since Lawrence was suffering from tuberculosis.[35] Aldington accompanied him as far as Toulon, where he parted with Lawrence—"a remarkable man, the most interesting human being I have ever known"—for the last time (*LL*, 333–34).

Aldington was enchanted with the natural beauty of the island. It was there that he began his first novel, *Death of a Hero*, and completed more than a fourth of it in a week and a half, though he had made several attempts to write the book since 1919. He was glad, however, that he had made no progress with it earlier, for it was published at the time that war novels were most popular. When he showed the partial manuscript to the Lawrences, D. H. was very scornful, but Frieda was pleased, and Aldington never forgot her encouragement. Far from feeling any resentment toward her husband, Aldington was so disgusted with the attacks of the English press on *Lady Chatterley's Lover* that he resolved to give up residence in England altogether; he no longer wished to associate with the kind of people who were trying to discredit Lawrence.

VI *The Expatriate*

At this time, in 1928, when Aldington rejected residence in England, he must have broken with Dorothy Yorke. They were still together during his sojourn at Port-Cros, but they probably separated before he returned to Paris. In any event, he began to have a passionate love affair around Christmas with "Brigit" Patmore (née Ethel Elizabeth Morrison-Scott), an Irishwoman who had married John Deighton Patmore, the grandson of Coventry Patmore, the poet.[36] Aldington had known her since 1912, when she was a member of Violet Hunt's literary circle. He had met her through a mutual acquaintance after leaving University College, London, and she in turn had introduced him to Pound and H. D. The four of them were constant companions in those days, and Aldington not only had continued to see her from time to time in the years that followed but had helped her find work as a translator after her separation from her husband who had suffered financial ruin in 1924.[37] She had also been one of his guests at Port-Cros,[38] but she had returned to England before joining him again in Paris. Though she was ten years older than Aldington (she was almost forty-seven and had two grown sons when the affair began), she has been described by various persons as a remarkably beautiful woman who always appeared to be much younger than her age. Neither of them was legally divorced (not until later did Aldington obtain a divorce from H. D.), but they were apparently very happy during the decade or so that they spent living and traveling together.[39]

Death of a Hero was only one of Aldington's publications in 1929.

In addition to *Remy de Gourmont: Selections from All His Works*, a new collection of his own verse and a poem called *The Eaten Heart* were issued by different publishers. In 1930, after a tour of Tunisia and Algeria, he began a second novel, *The Colonel's Daughter*, part of which he wrote while on the French Riviera and which he completed in Venice and Lecce. He explains his frequent change of residence by saying, "The farther I was from England and the more alien my surroundings, the more vividly I could picture English scenes and people" (*LL*, 364). Although the novel was not published until the following year, 1930 saw several of his works in print; including *A Dream in the Luxembourg* (a long poem written in 1928), *Roads to Glory* (a collection of short stories), and translations of Boccaccio's *Decameron* and Euripides' *Alcestis*.

Just before Christmas, 1930, Aldington left Lecce for Florence, where he renewed his friendship with Giuseppi ("Pino") Orioli whose close friend, the Scottish author Norman Douglas, he met. Aldington stayed more than a year in Florence, saw Douglas almost every day, and took great pleasure in the older man's conversation and companionship. To Aldington, "It did not trouble me in the least that I differed very strongly from Douglas on certain points of human conduct, wherein I did not and do not approve either his theory or his practice" (which is apparently an oblique reference to Douglas' homosexuality). At any rate, Aldington's glowing recollections of Douglas indicate that he sincerely admired the man for his culture, learning, and accomplishments (*LL*, 369).

In 1931, in addition to *The Colonel's Daughter*, Aldington produced his satire about T. S. Eliot, *Stepping Heavenward*, and a translation of Remy de Gourmont's *Letters to the Amazon*. In 1932 he published a second collection of short stories under the title of *Soft Answers*, plus an English version of *Aurelia* by Gerard de Nerval. To escape the interruptions of his work in Florence, he retired to the quiet of Anacapri in the spring of 1932. There he resumed work on a new novel, *All Men Are Enemies*, which he had begun in Florence, until his social obligations took him to the French Riviera in the summer. But he was glad to leave Italy, for he was depressed by the wretched condition of a people under Fascist rule. After 1932 he also gave up his frequent trips to Paris, perhaps to get away from the "world of pseudo-artistic fashion and trifling" (*LL*, 374) that annoyed him there. His novel *All Men Are Enemies* was published in 1933 (his only new book for that year), and the film rights were sold later to the motion-picture industry in Hollywood.[40]

By this time, Aldington was realizing more and more royalties from the work he had already done; and, while he did not cease to write, he was no longer dependent upon regular employment or publication. Indeed, by the end of 1926 he had begun to realize that he had increasingly more time and money for leisure and travel; and, as the years passed, he was prepared to take advantage of his opportunities to enjoy life. Since the spring of 1928, he had formed the habit of "writing all morning, excursions in the afternoon, and talk after dinner" (*LL*, 380)—a program that was a decided contrast to the one before his brief collapse two years earlier when he had "toiled madly, cut down . . . sleep and walks, and generally lived with an asceticism" he would "have mocked at in somebody else" (*LL*, 292). Furthermore, his increasing prosperity and leisure were largely responsible for his emergence as a novelist; for he had not been willing to take the risk of such a venture earlier.

In 1933 Aldington began making long tours of Spain and Portugal, continuing to visit those countries until late May, 1936, shortly before the Spanish Civil War began. He had also planned an extended tour of Eastern Europe, since he had invitations from the publishers of his novels in Czechoslovakia, Hungary, and Poland—and since he had "blocked" royalties in the last two countries and in the Soviet Union. In early June, 1934, he started out by automobile for Vienna; but he suffered a fractured kneecap in an accident soon after crossing the Swiss border into Austria and never completed the trip. While he was convalescing at Fontanella, the Austrian chancellor, Dollfuss, was assassinated by the Nazis. Aldington's books had already been banned in Germany, and he was soon informed that he was also unwelcome in Austria. He thus altered his plans and toured Alsace-Lorraine and the Pyrenees during the next few months, for his injury "had stopped all serious work" for the remainder of the year (*LL*, 397–98). Nevertheless, he had finished another novel, *Women Must Work*, early in the spring, and it was published the same year, 1934.

Aldington had hoped to spend the winter in a villa on the French Riviera, but the news of more political assassinations made him change his mind and go to England. Before reaching London, however, he injured his knee again and had to undergo a second operation and another tedious period of recovery. Since he had already resolved not to live in England and since he had now begun to feel uncomfortable on the Continent, he decided to experience life in North America and took a "banana boat" to the West Indies in early February, 1935:

I had given a lot of energy to the task of trying to fit myself to be a good European. . . . I perceived with dismay that there might very soon be no Europe in which one might try to be good. . . . Violent minorities were betraying and murdering all that had dignified their countries. Reluctantly and ruefully I had to admit that there was no longer anywhere in Europe I wanted to live in; and that there was no place for me among intellectual fanatics who were busy labelling themselves leftists and rightists, and who constantly summoned one to stand and deliver on one silly side or the other. (*LL*, 400)

Upon his arrival in the Caribbean, Aldington rented a bungalow on the island of Tobago, where he stayed for the rest of the winter and for all of the spring in order to allow his knee to heal properly. During the first part of his sojourn there, he worked very hard on two new books, *Artifex*, a collection of original essays, and *The Spirit of Place: An Anthology Compiled from the Prose of D. H. Lawrence*—both of which were published the same year, 1935, along with *Life Quest*, a long poem.

Brigit Patmore had been with Aldington all this time; and when they arrived in New York, they were joined by her eldest son, Derek, who was also a writer. Since Derek Patmore had been living in New York for some time, he was able to act as their guide and to introduce them to people.[41] Unlike many other English authors, Aldington refused to tour America as a lecturer; he preferred to see America on his own terms and at his own leisure. After about a month in the city, he moved to a quiet farmhouse on the Connecticut River where he apparently lived for several years—at least until 1940—although in the meantime he visited northern New England (and probably other parts of the United States). And he was speaking of his first months at Old Lyme, Connecticut,[42] when he wrote, "There, under the crystal-blue autumn sky, when the woods are aflame with colour and the light cold wind brings the first wild duck from Canada, I made up my mind that henceforth I would make my headquarters in America" (*LL*, 410).

At this point, Aldington's account of himself ends. Though his autobiography was published in 1941 (following partial serialization in *The Atlantic Monthly* in 1940), it provides very little information about his life and work after the autumn of 1935. In 1936, at least a part of which he spent in Europe, he had only one book issued, *Life of a Lady*, a play adapted (in collaboration with Derek Patmore) from one of his short stories; but he had a new novel published annually during the next three years: *Very Heaven* (1937), *Seven Against Reeves* (1938), and *Rejected Guest* (1939). He also produced a long poem, *The Crystal World*, in 1937, and a study of W. Somerset Maugham in 1939.

Prior to the American involvement in the war, Aldington made two long visits to Europe. The first occasion was to marry Netta McCulloch, a pretty Scottish woman who had formerly been the wife of Michael Patmore, Brigit's younger son;[43] and the second event was the birth of his daughter, Catherine, a year and a half later. By 1939, however, Aldington had declared his intention to make the United States his permanent home, probably for two major reasons: it was physically remote from a war which was threatening to destroy Europe; and it was a country where (at least for a time) he had finally "found English-speaking people who were unaffected, straightforward, and simply themselves, and took for granted that I should be the same, . . . a great relief" (*LL*, 238).

At this point, a gap occurs in the record of Aldington's life; but it is certain that Aldington resided in the United States during World War II,[44] and it is doubtful that he was able to venture very far beyond its borders until peace was declared. The war, moreover, does not appear to have been conducive to either his literary efforts or his appreciation of America and its people; and, while he was beginning at that time to focus his attention on biographical studies, he published few books from 1940 to 1945. These publications were *Life for Life's Sake*, his autobiography (1941); *The Viking Book of Poetry of the English-Speaking World*, an anthology (1941); *The Duke, Being an Account of the Life & Achievements of Arthur Wellington*, a biography (1943); and *A Wreath for San Gemignano*, a new version of one of his earlier translations (1945).

Around July, 1944, he moved to Los Angeles and rented an apartment on Sunset Strip, next door to Ciro's Restaurant. He remained in that city, where he was employed as a Hollywood script writer at a thousand dollars a week, until April, 1946, when he departed by automobile for New Orleans. From there he took a plane to Miami; he then flew on to Kingston, Jamaica; and he stayed there for a while before going to Paris later in the year.[45] These movements and his disillusionment with the United States may be accounted for in a letter which he wrote to his friend Herbert Read: "These people degenerate on acquaintance. . . . It is partly a difference of our temperaments, but partly also the result of residence, that I long ago ceased to expect any real contact or friendship with Americans, and lived with the landscape, the still extensive relics of primitive America. Rather as Lawrence did—except that I think his red Indians detestable and boring barbarians."[46] Though the cause of these reactions is not really known, Aldington's attitude toward Americans had obviously undergone a great change since the time he had spoken admiringly of them as an "unaffected, straightforward" people. It is idle to speculate whether the change was sudden or gradual, but the make-believe world of Hollywood would appear to be one of the least likely places where he might have found people with the qualities he admired.

VII *Last Years*

Upon arriving in Paris, Aldington lived for a time in a studio at 162 Boulevard du Montparnasse.[47] His publications for 1946 included *The Romance of Casanova* (a novel), *The Portable Oscar Wilde*, and a volume of translations, *Great French Romances*. In 1947 he moved to the Villa Aucassin at LeLavandou on the French Riviera and stayed there until after his separation from his wife Netta about 1950. She returned to England, but he apparently retained custody of their young daughter Catherine who remained "devoted" to a father who "worshipped" her.[48] He received the James Tait Black Memorial Prize in 1947 for his biography of the Duke of Wellington, and he published three books in 1948: *Jane Austen*, *Four English Portraits*, and *The Complete Poems of Richard Aldington*. Two more biographies followed, *The Strange Life of Charles Waterton* (1949) and *D. H. Lawrence: Portrait of a Genius But . . .* (1950). In 1950 he also edited *The Religion of Beauty: Selections from the Aesthetes*, compiled the *Selected Letters of D. H. Lawrence*, and wrote introductions to ten of Lawrence's books (two published by Heinemann and eight for the Penguin Books series).

After Aldington changed his residence to the Villa les Rosiers at Montpellier in 1951,[49] he produced no new books for the next three years; but he was working hard on a pair of biographies which were to have a profound effect on his reputation as a writer. These two books, published in 1954, were *Pinorman: Personal Recollections of Norman Douglas, Pino Orioli, and Charles Prentice* and *Lawrence L'Imposteur: T. E. Lawrence, The Legend and the Man* (reissued in 1955 as *Lawrence of Arabia: A Biographical Enquiry*). Aldington had already offended many people with his biography of D. H. Lawrence, and he made more enemies with his portrait of Douglas. But his exposure of the T. E. Lawrence legend, which was thoroughly investigated and documented, was even more severely attacked by the English press. Despite, a favorable article in 1957 by an old friend, Sir William Haley, who was now editor of *The Times*,[50] Aldington was ostracized by the English critics and soon saw most of his books go out of print in England. These circumstances had the unfortunate effect of relegating him to comparative obscurity and to financial distress for the remainder of his life.[51]

In France, however, Aldington's reputation was uninjured; he received the Prix de Gratitude Mistralienne in 1959 for his *Introduction to Mistral* (1956).[52] The same year, a younger friend from Australia, Alister Kershaw, who had been his private secretary and who had persuaded him to write the book on T. E. Lawrence,[53] gave Aldington his own small cottage, the Maison Sallé near Sury-en-Vaux in central France. There Aldington spent the last three years of his life, loved by his French neighbors. Though he did not travel much during those years, he made a few trips to the south of France to see his daughter, who was enrolled at the university in Aix-en-Provence, and to Switzerland to see H. D. and Winifred Ellerman ("Bryher") with whom he had reestablished friendships after his return to France.[54] He also visited Venice in 1961.[55] After 1957, when he published his final biographical studies, *Frauds* and *Portrait of a Rebel: The Life and Works of Robert Louis Stevenson*, he did very little writing, the most ambitious of his efforts being the *Larousse Encyclopedia of Mythology* (1959), which he translated in collaboration with Delano Ames.

Aldington's life, which had not been an entirely happy one, was additionally marred by his unexpected misfortunes toward its end. Nevertheless, he has been described as a cheerful man by several persons who knew him during his last years. Harry T. Moore, who notes that Aldington "was not at all frustrated and embittered," observed that "His wit was sharp, his tone cheerful."[56] To Sir Alec Randall, he was "gay" and "full of humour and kindliness."[57] Henry

Miller, who met him only once, found him moody but capable of being "jovial."[58] Thomas McGreevy, who had not seen him for many years, says that "he looked very well" appeared to be "as young and at least as debonair as he had . . . a quarter of a century earlier," and reminisced "light-heartedly" about the past.[59] Lawrence Durrell speaks of him as an "utterly delightful man" with a "truly endearing grumpiness" which he feigned "for the pleasure of making us laugh."[60] Frédéric-Jacques Temple remarks that his outward behavior did not betray "his difficulties, which he bore with a truly lordly stoicism and dignity."[61] And Alister Kershaw, who was probably closer to Aldington than any of the others, has this to say:

It was hopefully asserted from time to time that he had become "bitter" and "sour" as a result of the successful wrecking of his career. Some hope! Much he cared for the squeaks of a pack of sub-intellectuals in London pubs. It's amusing, too, that the little literary people, so repulsively jealous and mean-spirited themselves, should have affected to believe that Richard was "soured." He was, on the contrary, the least envy-ridden man I have ever encountered: at a time when he himself was going through the most difficult period of his existence, he was absolutely delighted with the success of Lawrence Durrell. His own situation was irrelevant when it was a question of saluting work that he felt to be good.[62]

These comments are, of course, extracts from eulogies written by Aldington's friends; but they must be weighed against the rancor of his enemies, who have attempted to dismiss him, without any apparent justification, as a bitter and malicious man.

To the very end, Aldington was active and seemed to be in "robust good health,"[63] but he is reported to have had "bouts of ill-health" throughout his life and "bronchial trouble" as he grew older.[64] In the summer of 1962, he accepted an invitation from the Soviet Writers' Union to visit Russia for three weeks. His reception in that country was overwhelming, and he received many tributes from Soviet readers, writers, and publishers while he was there. Accompanied by his daughter Catherine, he celebrated his seventieth birthday in Moscow and made excursions to Leningrad and Yasnaya Polyana, the site of Tolstoy's tomb.[65] About two weeks after his return to his cottage in France—still exuberant from the memory of his triumph in the Soviet Union—he suddenly became ill on the morning of July 27, 1962, and died about noon of the same day. Aldington was buried in the Sury-en-Vaux cemetery.[66]

CHAPTER 2

The Imagist

THE influence of Richard Aldington upon the development of modern poetry in both England and America has been acknowledged but not emphasized. Encyclopedias and literary histories mention the fact that he was one of the leaders of the imagist movement, but, apart from the studies of Glenn Hughes and Stanley Coffman, little attempt has been made to explain his specific contributions to this seminal movement which Hughes calls "the best-organized and most influential . . . since the activity of the pre-Raphaelites."[1] Though Aldington has been recognized as only a minor poet himself, he was a man who marched in the vanguard of perhaps the most important poetic revolution of the early twentieth century and who, at one time or other, was closely associated with many of the greatest literary figures in England and America.

In order to assess Aldington's place among the creators of the new poetry in the English language that was imagism, it is helpful to review the history of the movement. Hughes has traced its beginnings to T. E. Hulme, an Englishman whose interest in a philosophy of aesthetics led him to found the Poets' Club in London in 1908 and to become the "father of Imagism"[2] by writing a few verses which served as the earliest models for the new poetry. When the club was reorganized the following year, the members included Ezra Pound, Edward Storer, and F. S. Flint.[3] According to Flint, the group was strongly influenced by French symbolism and was experimenting with free verse, with Hebraic form, and with Japanese *haiku* and *tanka*; at the same time, Flint says, "There was also a lot of talk and practice among us, Storer leading it chiefly, of what we called the Image."[4]

Although Pound did not actually invent the term, he saved it from oblivion and was also the first to bring it to the attention of readers.[5] He did not, however, find entirely satisfactory models for the new poetry among his own writings or those of the other members of the short-lived club, for even Hulme's few lines had been written merely as examples to demonstrate a theory.[6] As Aldington himself has pointed out, it was more or less by chance that his own verses fulfilled Pound's requirements,[7] for he had not belonged to the earlier clubs and had developed independently as a poet through his own study of Greek, Latin, and French forms, just as H. D. had. While Pound undoubtedly exerted considerable influence on Aldington and H. D. during the early stages of the movement, his influence appears to have been restricted to guidance and criticism; and he obviously recognized qualities in their poems which he did not find in his own.

As for the poetry this group produced, H. D.'s poems have been generally recognized as the most perfect productions of the imagists; but Ezra Pound's initial leadership and shrewd critical judgment were indispensable to the founding of imagism as a real movement, and Amy Lowell's diplomacy and patronage were essential to the continuance of the movement until it was firmly established. But, throughout the development of the movement, Richard Aldington remained at the center as a poet, a critic, and a leader.[8] In fact, the 1915 anthology, *Some Imagist Poets*, also contained an unsigned preface by Aldington, with some revisions by Amy Lowell,[9] that explained the principles of imagism:

1. To use the language of common speech, but to employ always the exact word, not the nearly-exact, nor the merely decorative word.
2. To create new rhythms—as the expression of new moods—and not to copy old rhythms, which merely echo old moods. We do not insist upon "free verse" as the only method of writing poetry. We fight for it as for a principle of liberty. We believe that the individuality of a poet may often be better expressed in free verse than in conventional forms. In poetry, a new cadence means a new idea.
3. To allow absolute freedom in the choice of subject. It is not good art to write badly about aeroplanes and automobiles; nor is it necessarily bad art to write well about the past. We believe passionately in the artistic value of modern life, but we wish to point out that there is nothing so uninspiring nor so old-fashioned as an aeroplane of the year 1911.
4. To present an image (hence the name, imagist). We are not a school of painters, but we believe that poetry should render particulars exactly and not deal in vague generalities, however magnificent and sonorous. It is for this reason that we oppose the cosmic poet, who seems to us to shirk the real difficulties of his art.

5. To produce poetry that is hard and clear, never blurred nor indefinite.
6. Finally, most of us believe that concentration is of the very essence of poetry.[10]

I *The "Greek Dream"*

The first imagist poems by Aldington to be published as such were "Choricos," "To a Greek Marble," and "In the Old Garden" (originally "Au Vieux Jardin"). As in the case of most of the poems discussed in this and the next two chapters, they have been reprinted in *The Complete Poems of Richard Aldington* (1948).[11] "Choricos," a tribute to personified Death, is regarded by Glenn Hughes as "one of Aldington's most effective efforts to recapture the Hellenic mood"; and Hughes calls attention to the poem's "austere grace," its "coolness and dignity as of an Attic temple."[12] To illustrate this quality, he quotes the first lines:

> The ancient songs
> Pass deathward mournfully.
>
> Cold lips that sing no more, and withered wreaths,
> Regretful eyes, and drooping breasts and wings—
> Symbols of ancient songs,
> Mournfully passing
> Down the great white surges,
> Watched of none
> Save the frail sea-birds
> And the lithe pale girls,
> Daughters of Oceanus.   (*CP*, 21)

The poem contains a number of allusions to Greek mythology: "Oceanus," "Cimmerian dusk," "Proserpina, daughter of Zeus," "Phoebus Apollo" (*CP*, 21). Aldington justifies their use in this and other poems by what he calls a "sense of mystery"; and he explains, with a faint echo of D. H. Lawrence's theory of "spirit of place," that such poems reflect "the experience of certain places and times when one's whole nature seems to be in touch with a presence, a *genius loci*, a potency."[13] Whenever he employs "the word 'god' or 'gods' or the name of some Hellenic deity," he is "not indulging in a mythological flourish" but is referring "to the actual experience of some 'potency'."[14] At any rate, his attempt to convey a quasi-religious experience is very effective in the poem. Turning to the imagery, Hughes praises the "coloring and movement"[15] of the following lines:

> For silently
> Brushing the fields with red-shod feet,
> With purple robe
> Searing the grass as with a sudden flame,
> Death,
> Thou hast come upon us.   (*CP*, 21–22)

The influence of Algernon Swinburne on the poem is pointed out by Thomas McGreevy, who finds "Death in purple robe and red shoes . . . a horribly Pre-Raphaelite piece of imagining" and adds that "the Pre-Raphaelite pale woman (Swinburne's Proserpine) . . . lingered long" in Aldington's mind.[16] Indeed, the theme, the imagery, and the mythology of "Choricos" owe much to Swinburne's "Hymn to Proserpine" and "The Garden of Proserpine." Both "Choricos" and the "Hymn" are monodies that mourn the passing of the ancient gods and beliefs. In the "Hymn" Swinburne invokes the queen of the dead to "be near me now and befriend"; but, at the same time, he repudiates devotion to Aphrodite, with her "barren breasts of love," and to "Apollo, with hair and harpstring of gold,/ A bitter God to follow." These lines have their parallel in "Choricos," where the poet has been speaking of the realm of Proserpine: "And we turn from the Cyprian's breasts,/ And we turn from thee,/ Phoebus Apollo,/ And we turn from the music of old" (*CP*, 21). Moreover, certain similarities exist in the descriptions of the sea and the land; Aldington's "slim colourless poppies" (*CP*, 22) in the garden of Death have their counterpart in the "bloomless buds of poppies" in the "Garden of Proserpine"; but in the "Hymn" these poppies "are as sweet as the rose in our world."

Except for alliteration, which is employed more sparingly in Aldington's poem than in the "Hymn," the prosody of "Choricos" appears to owe nothing to Swinburne or the Pre-Raphaelites. McGreevy maintains that Aldington, through his use of free verse, has "gained over Swinburne . . . in the more natural, less mechanical rhythm" and has "won something of the subtle Greek harmony that is independent of any such mechanical element as rhyme."[17]

According to Stanley Coffman, Aldington's "unit of rhythm in his early poems is unquestionably the unit of conversation, the lines terminating with a voice and a sense stop, but his reliance upon a constant to unify a poem is not so easily discernible." With reference to an analysis of this poem by Yvor Winters, who cannot identify any "pattern" after the seventh line, Coffman indicates that "nearly one-third of the lines begin with an anapestic foot, whose movement is retarded by frequent use of unaccented syllables whose quantitative value approximates that of the accented syllable," and that "groups of lines at least are unified by a pattern of initial reiteration which has the effect of a constant." He concludes that even though such "devices . . . do not give a single unity, they give cohesiveness enough to avoid violation of the poem's clear unity of feeling," and he adds, "Other poems show a similarly free expression."[18]

If "Choricos" is largely derivative with respect to subject matter, Aldington had found a new way to express the old material. A related poem is his "Hermes, Leader of the Dead," in which not only the theme but also the mood and imagery are very similar to those of the first poem. As in "Choricos," the only innovation appears to be the use of free verse, for the lines continue to reflect the soft, traditional imagery of late Victorian poetry—a characteristic that appears in poems in which Aldington is dealing with subjects from Greek and Roman mythology. In "Hermes," the poet also fails to present any vivid images; he contents himself with the creation of a vague, nostalgic mood. In the lines, "Eos/ That maiden whiter than Narcissus" (CP, 30), mere whiteness does not describe either a god or a goddess; and "midday heat" and "sea-winds rustling across the vineyards" (CP, 30) do not give the reader a picture of a landscape.

The reader also finds it difficult to visualize the scene in Hades which is suggested by the "dark blue ways," the "heavy bowed gold blossoms," and the "very grey sky" (CP, 30). Simple colors and intensives are not enough—the fragmentary details must be more graphic or striking to evoke a good image. Furthermore, the use of an unusual mythological name, Orcus, adds little to the effect of the lines. Orcus is a Roman term for Hades, the Greek underworld which lies beyond Ocean and the sunless country of the Cimmerians, both of which are mentioned in "Choricos." The spirits of the dead themselves inhabit the Meadow of Asphodel, and Aldington describes their existence in another poem, "Reflections":

> Ghost moths hover over asphodel;
> Shades, once Lais' peers
> Drift past us;
> The mist is grey. (*CP*, 40)

In this passage, which produces a rather good image of the shadowy abode of the dead, the outlines of the figures are meant to be pale and indistinct; and the gray mist reinforces a grayness which is already suggested by the shades of dead beauties drifting among the lusterless flowers and ghostly moths.[19]

In "Lesbia" Aldington continues to lament the passing of the gods from human lives and affairs: "And Picus of Mirandola is dead;/ And all the gods they dreamed and fabled of,/ . . . And through it all I see your pale Greek face" (*CP*, 28). The "pale Greek face"—the "Greek dream"—remains to haunt the poet and to excite his imagination. Though the gods are dead, their ghosts still possess a certain "potency" for him, which he expresses in "Lemures." They do not trouble him by day, "But in the dusk," he says, "I am afraid of their rustling,/ Of their terrible silence,/ The menace of their secrecy" (*CP*, 29). The poet, however, does not content himself with elegies for the dead gods; he invokes their spirits to come to life once again.

"To a Greek Marble" takes the form of a prayer: "Potnia, Potnia,/ White grave goddess,/ Pity my sadness,/ O Silence of Paros":

> I have whispered thee in thy solitudes
> Of our loves in Phrygia,
> The far ecstasy of burning noons
> When the fragile pipes
> Ceased in the cypress shade,
> And the brown fingers of the shepherd
> Moved over slim shoulders;
> And only the cicada sang. (*CP*, 24)

Coffman cites this poem as an example of Aldington's "feeling for the beauty of natural objects, the human body, or physical passions, which he found best expressed through the art and mythology of classical Greece." Here, the critic points out, the poet "recreates the intense reaction to physical beauty which must have moved the sculptor" by presenting "a succession of images which make not only pictorial, but aural and tactile appeals: fragile pipes, cicada song, brown fingers moving over slim shoulders, the 'sun upon thy breasts.' " He also indicates that the piece "does not rely upon metaphor but bases its appeal upon the cumulative effect . . . of separate images."[20]

These observations by Coffman need some qualification. While Aldington does present more than one image in the poem, a single scene is suggested by the lines quoted above. Furthermore, this image is the only well-developed one in the poem. There is nothing specific about the "garments and decorum" (CP, 24) which are mentioned in the preceding stanza, nor about the hills in the last stanza where the "lisp of reeds" and "sun upon thy breasts" (CP, 24) are simply tantalizing fragments of images. The one complete image of the lovers is, of course, a choice one; but here, as in the rest of the poem, the diction and style seem to echo earlier poets rather than to show evidence of a new vocabulary or manner of expression. The archaic pronouns ("thou," "thee," "thy") are especially obvious as elements of the language of traditional poetry, as are phrases such as "lover of aforetime crying to thee," "whispered thee in thy solitudes," and "far ecstasy of burning noons" (CP, 24). In three out of four stanzas, Aldington tends to ignore his own rule that the poet should not sacrifice particulars for "sonorous" generalities; and even his commitment to free verse is ignored to some extent. Coffman mentions the fact that the first stanza conforms to a "traditional pattern," but he also remarks that, "From these carefully measured lines, it proceeds to others that have no immediately recognizable measure, but nevertheless show a kind of organization, stanza 2 being based upon a principle of balance between lines 5 and 6 and lines 7 and 8, with a ninth line which, repeated at the close of the poem, has the effect of a refrain."[21] It may be concluded, then, that although traditional measures are present in the poem, they are not a predominant feature of the overall metrical structure.

A similar poem, "At Mitylene," shows no deviation from a free-verse form, but its images are less evocative than that of the lovers discussed in "To a Greek Marble". "At Mitylene" opens with a summons: "O Artemis,/ Will you not leave the dark fastness/ And set your steel-white foot upon the foam" (CP, 26). The resemblance of the rhythms to those of biblical prose is noted by Coffman, who explains that the lines are "held together by co-ordination of sentence units and by repetition of the words in these units which emphasize their parallel structure."[22] This technique may be illustrated by the following lines:

> For these women have laid out a purple cloth,
> And they have builded you an altar
> Of white shells for the honey,
> They have taken the sea grass for garlands
> And cleansed their lips with the sea.
> ....
> And remember us—
> We, who have grown weary even of music,
> We, who would scream behind the wild dogs of Scythia. (*CP*, 26)

Artemis and Potnia are related goddesses, but the latter does not share the quality of chastity, which is also an attribute of Death in "Choricos." The poet's attitude toward the two goddesses is therefore quite different: his feeling for Potnia is physical, a longing for the beautiful body of a woman; but his feeling for Artemis is spiritual, a reverence for the classical beauty which she symbolizes. Aldington also appears to be perfectly sincere in his attempt to evoke "the actual experience of some 'potency,' " as he himself calls it; for he employs biblical prose rhythms in order to impart a genuine tone of reverence to the lines.

The "potency" of the ancient gods is expressed in another poem, "In the Via Sistina." The poet is fascinated by the beauty of an Italian prostitute, whose dark features remind him of "the face of Isis" (*CP*, 35). According to Greek myth, the Egyptian goddess Isis was once the mortal Io, whom Aldington invokes in "Bromios," one of several poems that sing the praises of the Greek and Italian deities of nature. "Bromios," subtitled "A Frieze in the Vatican," depicts the revels of the woodland spirits and human worshipers of Dionysus. The central figure of the scene is Io, the paramour of Zeus who was transformed into a heifer in order to hide her from Hera's jealousy. The fauns and satyrs have burst upon her unawares:

> The withered bonds are broken.
> The waxed reeds and the double pipe
> Clamour about me;
> The hot wind swirls
> Through the red pine trunks.
>
> Io! The fauns and the satyrs.
> The touch of their shagged curled fur
> And blunt horns.

> They have wine in heavy craters
> Painted black and red;
> Wine to splash on her white body.
>
> Io!
> She shrinks from the cold shower—
> Afraid, afraid!
> Let the Maenads break through the myrtles
> And the boughs of the rhododaphnai.
> Let them tear the quick deer's flesh.
> Ah, the cruel exquisite fingers.
>
> Io!
> I have brought you the brown clusters,
> The ivy-boughs and pine-cones.
> Your breasts are cold sea-ripples,
> But they smell of the warm grasses.
> Throw wide the chiton and the peplum,
> Maidens of the dew,
> Beautiful are your bodies, O Maenads,
> Beautiful the sudden folds,
> The vanishing curves of white linen
> About you.
>
> Io!
> Hear the rich laughter of the forest,
> The cymbals,
> The trampling of the panisks and the centaurs.   (CP, 36–37)

This highly animated scene—full of frenzy and terror—the poet has observed in a piece of ancient art. By placing Io at the center of the group—by focusing the attention of the revelers upon her—Aldington sustains and develops his image, which is enhanced rather than weakened by the variety of movement and activity. The poem, characterized by straightforward description, has few generalities and few embellishments of figurative language; and perhaps it is just as well that the poet is sparing in his use of figures of speech, since the metaphor, "Your breasts are cold sea-ripples," seems a bit labored. The exclamation of Io's name at the beginning of each stanza is effective, for it emphasizes not only the unity of the

scene which revolves around her but also the unrestrained wildness
of the orgy and the fear that it inspires in her.

Less effective is the comment "Afraid, afraid!" Io has already
demonstrated her fear by shrinking from the fauns and satyrs, and
some other detail concerning the reason for her fright would better
express her emotion. Certain references to the Maenads are similarly vague. The poet might have chosen more descriptive adjec-
tives for their fingers than "cruel" and "exquisite," and he might
have described the beauty of their bodies as well as their garments,
instead of merely saying that they are "beautiful." While there is
nothing particularly novel or unusual about the imagery, the poem
as a whole does present a vivid and stirring scene. Appeals to the
different senses are more numerous than in "To a Greek Marble,"
and they include smell in addition to sight, touch, and hearing.
Much of the vigor of the lines, moreover, may be attributed to the
new cadences which the poet has discovered in his experimentation
with free verse.

In "Reflections," a poem containing a variety of images, Aldington
mentions the nymphs, "the golden-haired revellers" of "the mad
procession" (*CP*, 40) which always accompanies Dionysus in his
wanderings. They are also followers of Pan, god of the shepherds
and hills; and the poem "Stele" depicts sadness in the midst of the
gaiety and frenetic activity of the revelers. "Stele" opens with "Pan,
O Pan,/ The oread weeps in the stony olive-garden" (*CP*, 27); and
the lament is repeated at the beginning of alternate stanzas. Aldington develops the image of the garden:

> There bloom the fragile
> Blue-purple wind-flowers,
> There the wild fragrant narcissus
> Bends by the grey stones. . . . .
> She heeds not the moss-coloured lizards
> And crocus-yellow butterflies. (*CP*, 27)

This poem is only one of many pieces which reveal the poet's love of
nature and his delight in its beauty; and his sensitivity to the beauty
of flowers is particularly evident in the passage quoted above. Spec-
ification of color is precise in the lines describing the lizards and
butterflies; for instead of simply saying that they are green and

yellow, the poet describes them as "moss-coloured" and "crocus-yellow." The lines that follow these explain the cause of the weeping nymph's sorrow. A member of Pan's riotous troupe, she is heartbroken at the loss of "her reed-pipe/ That was the crying of the wind,/ Her pipe that was the singing/ Wind of the mountain," for the god has accidently "broken her little reed" with his "stamping hoofs" (*CP*, 27).

In "Argyria," Pan grieves for a nymph who has just died. Although the poem focuses upon her, she remains a rather hazy and indistinct figure. Although this defect appears to violate a cardinal principle of imagism—"To produce poetry that is hard and clear, never blurred nor indefinite"—the apparent violation is probably intentional, as in the description of Hades in "Reflections." Even in life, the nymphs are represented in mythology as airy and elusive beings; and, when they die, their bodies evidently fade away into the natural surroundings they inhabited. The imagery of the poem succeeds very well in conveying these impressions. The versification involves a combination of free and traditional measures, and the traditional ones are most noticeable in the tenth and eleventh lines, where the fundamental rhythm is iambic pentameter (with variations upon the iambic pattern), and in the last two lines, each of which contains four beats and a similar pattern of stressed syllables.

Two monologues spoken by fauns—"The Faun Captive" and "The Faun Sees Snow for the First Time"—show the same vigorous exuberance which is present in "Bromios." They are reminiscent of Stéphane Mallarmé's "L'Après-Midi d'un Faune," but they lack the dreamlike quality of that French symbolist composition and are less turgid in thought and style. "The Faun Sees Snow for the First Time" begins with an oath:

> Zeus,
> Brazen-thunder-hurler,
> Cloud-whirler, son-of-Kronos,
> Send vengeance on these Oreads
> Who strew
> White frozen flecks of mist and cloud
> Over the brown trees and the tufted grass. . . .   (*CP*, 39)

The simple creature's rage and confusion are amusing, as are his antics when he tries to cope with the situation:

> Dis and Styx!
> When I stamp my hoof
> The frozen-cloud-specks jam into the cleft
> So that I reel upon two slippery points. . . .   (*CP*, 39)

The speaker in "The Faun Captive" is wiser, but he is as wild and uninhibited as the other one. Although the ancient gods are still very much alive in the poem, their power and influence among men have begun to wane; for men neither regard them with awe nor treat them with respect. When the faun opens his monologue with a carefully reasoned argument against the injustice of his predicament, he first notes that "A god's strength lies/ More in the fervour of his worshippers/ Than in his own divinity" (*CP*, 69). As he ponders the change that has taken place, he notes that there is no longer anyone "who twines/ Red wool and threaded lilies round the brows/ Of my neglected statues," nor who "seeks my aid/ To add skill to the hunter's hand/ Or save some pregnant ewe or bitch/ Helpless in travail" (*CP*, 69). There is a dignity—even a noble quality—in the tone of the faun's complaint:

> I that should have been dreaded in wan recesses,
> Worshipped in high woods, a striker of terror
> To the wayfarer in lonely places,
> I, a lord of golden flesh and dim music,
> I, a captive and coarsely derided!   (*CP*, 69)

The faun's chagrin at his loss of honor and freedom finally gives way to quiet rage. He has strength enough yet to break his bonds and "kill, kill, kill in sharp revenge," to escape to the hills and "the unploughed lands no foot oppresses,/ The lands that are free, being free of man." Since he is a demigod, he has the power to aid men and has gladly bestowed favors in return for their homage; but, since his own welfare is not dependent upon their goodwill, he can destroy them with impunity if they offend him. This situation is not the case with the mortal poet in "Captive," who must suffer injustice without recourse or hope of escape except in death:

> They have torn the gold tettinx
> From my hair;

> And wrenched the bronze sandals
> From my ankles.
> . . . .
> I, who was free, am a slave;
> The Muses have forgotten me,
> The gods do not hear me.   (*CP*, 68)

The Complete Poems does not include anything from *The Love of
Myrrhine and Konallis* (1917),[23] a collection of forty separate but
closely related poems that contain abundant allusions to Greek
mythology and that are arranged in a sequence which tells a sort of
story of the relationship between two imaginary young women of
ancient Greece. In the first, Konallis, a nymphlike goat-girl of
Corinth, speaks of her first meeting with the beautiful hetaera Myrrhine; and the pieces that follow offer a panorama of scenes in the
development of their love affair. In some, the speaker is Konallis; in
others, Myrrhine; and occasionally the two women speak in unison.

The majority of these pieces contain images which are comparable
to many found in *The Complete Poems*. Hughes, who describes the
style of *Myrrhine and Konallis* as "akin to Mr. Aldington's translations from Anyte of Tegea, Anacreon, and Meleager," points out
that the poems "are rhetorical, archaic, and richly colored"—that
their "cadences are long and voluptuous," their "imagery weighted
with ornament."[24] He selects "Morning," the third poem in the
series, as an example:

> Hierocleia, bring hither my silver vine-
>   leaf carved armlet and the mirror
>   graven with two Maenads,
> For my heart is burned to dust with
>   longing for Konallis;
> And this is the silver armlet which
>   pressed into her side when I held her,
> And before this mirror she bound up
>   her golden hyacinth-curled hair. . . .   (*MK*, 19)

Once again, it is difficult to find anything original in the imagery,
which is very appealing without being conspicuously unconven-
tional. There is a charm in the description of the "silver vine-leaf
carved armlet" and of the "golden hyacinth-curled hair"; but the
metaphor of a heart "burned to dust with longing" sounds rather

stale. Specimens of the figurative language of some of the other poems may also be cited. Delicate visual images are suggested by "pear-pointed breasts" (*MK*, 25),[25] "oleander-tipped breasts blossoming beneath your thin robe" (*MK*, 27), and "swallow-wing-sailed barque" (*MK*, 49). Although little novelty exists in any of these phrases, certain others appear to be especially trite, such as "sweet-breathing meadows" (*MK*, 40), "the lamp of my joy is quenched in a black pool of sadness" (*MK*, 36), and the more elaborate conceit of "the frail spirit that leaped and mingled with your spirit, like two flames" (*MK*, 61–62).

Of course, it is not fair to a poet to quote a few words or phrases out of context, nor to judge a series of poems by one example, for the total effect of *Myrrhine and Konallis* is more impressive than these brief quotations would indicate. May Sinclair acknowledges that "the love is Lesbian," but she insists that "Aldington has kept for us its pagan innocence and candour, its mortal pathos, and left us no image that is not beautiful."[26] It is curious, however, that Aldington could have written so tenderly of a homosexual relationship between women when he always strongly disapproved of the same practice among men. Sinclair continues, "The figures, exquisite and fragile, pass shining as in some processional frieze of marble overlaid by gold, washed clean by the light of a world too remote, too long dead to excite our repulsion or our blame: a world not quite real."[27]

This evaluation is a good one of the impressions which the poems communicate to the reader, but Sinclair seems to go too far when she says that Aldington has created "a sequence of the most exquisite love poems in the language, poems that, if he had never written another line, ought to be enough to secure for him a high and permanent place in literature."[28] She would have done well if she had recognized the same weakness that she notes in the other poems which express Aldington's "Greek dream." With particular reference to "Stele," "Choricos," "Argyria," "In the Via Sistina," and "To a Greek Marble," she indicates that the poet has been born too late; that "he should have been young when Sappho or Anyte of Tegea were young"; for "half of him is not Greek, and it brings into his poetry an element which is not Greek, a pain, a dissatisfaction, a sadness that the purely Greek soul did not know," a "sad modernity into the heart of his Greek world."[29]

Aside from *Myrrhine and Konallis*, the poems examined thus far are among those which served as models for the imagist movement;

but they are not always perfectly consistent in fulfilling the requirements set forth by the poet and his colleagues. In considering such inconsistencies, one must remember that mere observance of a set of rules is no guarantee of high quality in a poem and that those poems which adhere most closely to imagist principles are not necessarily superior to some of the others in conveying a total impression. One must also bear in mind that, according to his own testimony, Aldington was not trying to write "flawless" imagist poetry. Moreover, even though he is guilty of certain infractions of the rules, he seldom strays so far that a poem becomes unrecognizable as a product of the movement.

A number of these violations of imagist principles have already been discussed. Instead of presenting a single image, Aldington frequently presents a series of images. Even "Stele," with its exquisite image of the garden, shifts to a different mood and scene midway in the poem—from the oread weeping alone to the lighthearted nymphs and fauns who have abandoned her. Again, in spite of the hardness and clarity of many of the images and ideas, some tend to be rather blurred or indefinite. The blurred image has been defended in the discussion of "Argyria" and in "Reflections" which describes the land of the dead, for the poet has employed it to produce special effects. But such an image cannot be so easily justified in such poems as "To a Greek Marble" and "Hermes, Leader of the Dead" because the images simply lack adequate development. The weakness of some of the images in these poems and others may be attributed to Aldington's failure to conform to another of the principles stated in the preface to the 1915 imagist anthology, *Some Imagist Poets:* "to employ always the *exact* word, not the nearly-exact, nor the merely decorative word."

While Aldington's choice of words is often very effective in creating the desired mood and imagery, analysis has shown that this is not always the case. His use of merely decorative words has also been pointed out, and to these may be added the Greek term "tettinx" (*CP*, 68) in the first line of "Captive," since it was apparently borrowed to lend a note of exoticism to an otherwise unremarkable poem. The poet's choice of metaphor is not always a happy one, either. The most infelicitous one is probably found in "Lemures" in which he describes the sun as "A gay child that bears a white candle" (*CP*, 29), for the flame of a mere candle is much too feeble to be compared with the brilliance of the sun. In addition, because his poems often contain passages which are diffuse, repetitive, and rhapsodic, Aldington violates the rules of "concentration," the avoidance of "vague generalities," and the use of "the language of common speech." This violation is most evident whenever the poet fails to create a vivid image—or any image at all, for that matter. Finally, although occasional lines or stanzas in some of the poems do conform to traditional metrical patterns, they are never allowed to dominate the rhythm of any poem as a whole; Aldington remains quite faithful to the principle of free verse. Indeed, his use of free verse often permits him to avoid the "nearly-exact" word which might have been required by the rhyme or meter of another form of verse.

II Haiku *and Other Early Images*

The influence of Japanese poetry is conspicuous in some of Aldington's early poems which deal with contemporary subjects. As noted at the beginning of this chapter, Ezra Pound and F. S. Flint had been experimenting with *haiku* and *tanka* before the establishment of imagism as a movement; two other imagists, Amy Lowell and John Gould Fletcher, later shared Pound's interest in these Japanese forms;[30] and Aldington amused himself in the trenches during the war by writing *haiku*.[31] As Hughes says, "Japanese poetry is often pure imagism, and above all other types of poetry it aims at the creation of mood";[32] and Coffman reminds the reader that Aldington frequently uses images in a particular way that Pound suggested: "by sudden and apt comparison to communicate 'an intellectual and emotional complex in an instant of time.' "[33] The method to which Pound refers is one that Harold G. Henderson describes in *An Introduction to Haiku* as "the 'principle of internal comparison' in which the differences are just as important as the likenesses" in a Japanese *haiku*.[34] In addition, Henderson maintains that a *haiku* "is a poem," and that "being a poem it is intended to express and to evoke emotion," a matter which has often been misunderstood by British and American writers, for "it has been the custom in the past to translate 'haiku' into 'epigram,' and this is quite misleading."[35]

While any "perfect" *haiku* or *tanka* does not appear among Aldington's *Complete Poems*, a number of his verses resemble the Japanese forms in certain respects. Like the other imagists, including Pound and Amy Lowell, Aldington probably had an imperfect understanding of the principles of Japanese poetry, for he does not consistently meet the conditions insisted upon by the masters of the verse which he more or less consciously imitates. He does not observe the five-seven-five syllable pattern for the *haiku* or the five-seven-five-seven-seven pattern for the *tanka*, which were fundamental requirements for Japanese poetry. The Japanese *haiku*, moreover, must always suggest one of the four seasons, and it rarely deals with the subject of love, although love is a common subject for the *tanka*. Such conventions, however, are obviously less important than the creation of images which evoke a mood or emotion, and Aldington's verses should be judged accordingly. Without trying to determine the more far-reaching effects of Japanese poetry upon his longer poems at this time, one may readily observe the influence upon the shorter ones and decide whether they are "poems" or only "epigrams."

One group of poems is called "Epigrams," and the first has the subtitle of "New Love":

> She has new leaves
> After her dead flowers,
> Like the little almond tree
> Which the frost hurt.   (*CP*, 32)

Aldington has modestly labeled this piece an "epigram," and, unfortunately, it is little more than just that. The first two lines do not contain a clear image: "new leaves" and "dead flowers" are general terms which do not convey specific color, shape, or species. Although it is evident that the poet intends that the reader should visualize the woman in the image of the almond tree, the presentation does not effectively accomplish this. When the skillful Japanese poet compares two images in a *haiku*, he has the lesser image evoke the greater one;[36] therefore, in "New Love," the tree should evoke the woman, since the woman is apparently Aldington's chief concern in the poem. A reversal of the lines (and therefore the images), without any modification of the words, should sharpen the image of the woman:

> Like the little almond tree
> Which the frost hurt,

> She has new leaves
> After her dead flowers.

The use of simile and the mixture of simile and metaphor,[37] although uncharacteristic of Japanese *haiku*,[38] seem to be appropriate and effective in the poem.

The second poem, "October," also employs a simile:

> The beech-trees are silver
> For lack of the tree's blood;
> At your kiss my lips
> Become like the silver beech-leaves.   (*CP*, 32)

Unlike the previous poem, this one seems to explain too much; the reader is not required to make a "leap of imagination" between the two images.[39] If the poem is judged by other standards, however, it compares in quality with some of the finest Japanese *tanka*. Take for example this translation of a *tanka* from the early tenth-century *Kokinshū*:

> Like the ice which melts
> When spring begins
> Not leaving a trace behind,
> May your heart melt toward me.[40]

From the standpoint of originality and imagery, this verse is not superior to Aldington's poem; on the contrary, "October" contains the clearer image. It is less easy to determine which of the two poems is the more effective in evoking emotion through the particular choice of simile.

In addition to his "Epigrams," Aldington has included two other sets of short verses, both entitled "Images," in the first section of his *Complete Poems*. As in the case of "October," these poems are probably better compared with Japanese *tanka* rather than with *haiku*. The following are from the first set:

1

> Like a gondola of green scented fruits
> Drifting along the dark canals of Venice,

You, O exquisite one,
Have entered into my desolate city.

2

The blue smoke leaps
Like swirling clouds of birds vanishing,
So my love leaps towards you,
Vanishes and is renewed.

5

The red deer are high on the mountain,
They are beyond the last pine-trees,
And my desires have run with them.   (*CP*, 38)

In numbers 1 and 5, a single image evokes an expressed thought or feeling, instead of another image which only implies the meaning through association; and number 2 employs two images to the same end. The poem below is from the other set of "Images":

You are beautiful
As a straight red foxglove
Among green plants;
I stretched out my hand to caress you:
It is blistered by the envious nettles.   (*CP*, 63)

Simile and metaphor combine in this piece to produce a simple but satisfactory image and meaning.

A somewhat longer poem, "Evening," also reflects a measure of the spirit and imagery found in Japanese poetry: the structure of the poem and the presentation of the images bear a marked, if possibly accidental, resemblance to Japanese *haikai*, or "free linked-verse." This form of poetry consists of the repetition of two basic elements, an opening *hokku* of three lines, followed by a two-line verse which contains a related thought or image. *Hokku* is simply another word for *haiku*, and the two are identical in all respects except that the latter term refers to an independent poem rather than to a component of a series of linked verses.[41] The last two lines (normally composed of seven syllables each) of the five-line group likewise complete a *tanka*, which again would be the proper term if the image of the two-line verse were not linked to another *hokku* in a continuing series that repeats the same pattern. In Aldington's "Evening":

> The chimneys, rank on rank,
> Cut the clear sky;
> The moon
> With a rag of gauze about her loins
> Poses among them, an awkward Venus—
>
> And here am I looking wantonly at her
> Over the kitchen sink.   (*CP*, 48)

The image of the moon is clearly linked to the image of the chimneys silhouetted against the sky, just as the image of the poet standing over his kitchen sink is linked to that of the moon; but the first and third images are related to each other only through the link provided by the moon image, and this conforms with the aims of the Japanese *haikai* poet. The reference to the moon and the microcosmic-macrocosmic comparison of man with moon also belong to the Japanese poetic tradition, even though their expression in the poem is by no means purely Japanese in character.

The first five stanzas of "London: May 1915" offer another example of *haikai* in English. It may be of interest to note here that the first two stanzas contain exactly seventeen syllables (though not in the traditional five-seven-five order), a basic requirement for Japanese *haiku* or *hokku*. As before, however, it is far more important to determine the quality of the images and their function in the poem than it is to count lines or syllables, although it is obvious that their number must be confined to certain limits:

> Glittering leaves
> Dance in a squall;
> Behind them bleak immoveable clouds.
>
> A church spire
> Holds up a little brass cock
> To peck at the blue wheat fields.
>
> Roofs, conical spires, tapering chimneys,
> Livid with sunlight, lace the horizon.

> A pear-tree, a broken white pyramid
> In a dingy garden, troubles me
> With ecstasy.
>
> At night, the moon, a pregnant woman,
> Walks cautiously over the slippery heavens.   (*CP*, 51)

The above images are not as skillfully linked together as those in "Evening," but a similarly weak linkage is also frequently found in Japanese *haikai*. While "blue" wheat fields would make no sense unless the reader were aware in advance that the apparent color is the result of an overcast sky, some of the images could be placed in a different order without essentially altering their cumulative effect, for only the title of the poem indicates that they are all aspects of a larger scene. The most striking image in the series is that of the moon; but the most genuine *haiku*, by Japanese standards, among all of Aldington's poems is probably found in the first stanza in which tiny leaves flutter briefly against the background of an awesome sky.

III *Love and Hate*

Aldington has been able to absorb and express in his own way the essence of Greek and Japanese poetry. The poems on subjects from Greek and Roman mythology, as well as the short Japanese-like verses on subjects from his own world, are among the best of the poet's earliest work. According to Coffman, however, when Aldington describes "contemporary scenes" in some of the other poems, he does "not always adequately objectify his attitude toward them." Coffman asserts that both "Childhood" and "Eros and Psyche" lack "successful poetic statement because the poet never transcends his personal distaste for his material."[42] This inability is certainly true of "Childhood," which is in large part a rather puerile and intemperate tirade. The poet begins by complaining, "The bitterness, the misery, the wretchedness of childhood/ Put me out of love with God" (*CP*, 55). Many of the lines that follow are very prosaic:

> I hate that town;
> I hate the town I lived in when I was little;
> I hate to think of it.
> . . . .
> There was nothing to see,

> Nothing to do,
> Nothing to play with. . . . (CP, 56–58)

One must agree that such lines can hardly be called "successful poetic statement," and they do appear to mar the one good image in "Childhood":

> Somebody found my chrysalis
> And shut it in a match-box.
> My shrivelled wings were beaten,
> Shed their colours in dusty scales
> Before the box was opened
> For the moth to fly.
> And then it was too late,
> Because the beauty a child has,
> And the beautiful things it learns before its birth,
> Were shed, like moth scales, from me. (CP, 55)

Aldington returns to the image of the captive moth in another stanza, and he uses it once more in the last four lines of the poem; but its effect is lost in the intervening invective and autobiographical scenes.

In "Eros and Psyche," on the other hand, the image of the two immortal lovers in the squalid setting of a manufacturing center is quite moving. Although Aldington restrains his bitterness, the predominant emotion is one of sorrow. He maintains an aesthetic distance from his subject by expressing his personal feelings in a less direct manner, by employing irony instead of invective to make his point:

> In a dull old yard near Camden Town,
> Which echoes with the rattle of cars and 'buses
> And freight-trains, puffing steam and smoke and dirt
> To the steaming sooty sky—
> There stands an old and grimy statue,
> . . . .
> Eros, naked, with his wings stretched out
> Just lighting down to kiss her on the lips. (CP, 52)

The poet declares that the divine pair "should stand in a sun-lit room/ Hung with deep purple" or "in a garden leaning above Corinth,/ Under the ilexes and cypresses,/ Very white against a very blue sky" (*CP*, 53). He contends that, if they must grow "hoary, if they must grow old," their aging should be hallowed by "lichens and softly creeping moss" (*CP*, 53), not profaned by layers of soot and dirt; and an extra touch is added to the irony by the contrast of a nearby statue honoring a grim-faced hero of the industrial revolution. Aldington's regret in this poem, as in "Childhood," is that so much beauty is spoiled by philistine obtuseness and negligence. He cannot resist the temptation to include unnecessary comments on the scene, but his exercise of restraint and his production of a more unified image combine to make "Eros and Psyche" a poignant statement of his impressions. Aldington is at his best when he does not become such an angry young man that he forgets his responsibilities as a poet.

Among Aldington's earliest poems, only two others seem to display unbridled anger or bitterness. "In the Tube," which is clearly a splenetic outburst, the poet is staring at the passengers on the opposite bench of his car in the subway. He sees a "row of hard faces,/ Immobile," a "row of eyes,/ Eyes of greed, of pitiful blankness, of plethoric complacency," which stare back at him—and such eyes are more than he can bear: "Antagonism,/ Disgust,/ Immediate antipathy,/ Cut my brain, as a dry sharp reed/ Cuts a finger./ I surprise the same thought/ In the brasslike eyes:/ '*What right have you to live?*' " (*CP*, 49). The lack of objectivity in the poem is apparent, for Aldington does not really try to understand the reactions of the other people in the car. If he glares at them with hatred and revulsion, it is natural that they will reply with frowns. There is also no reason to believe that they share his thought: "What right have you to live?" They are probably only thinking: "What is the matter with you?" The last lines of "Cinema Exit" are equally misanthropic: "Millions of human vermin/ Swarm sweating/ Along the night-arched cavernous roads./ (Happily rapid chemical processes/ Will disintegrate them all.)" (*CP*, 48).

But Aldington can love as passionately as he can hate. Fortunately, love is the more enduring passion in his poetry, and no better expression of the young poet's love for other human beings can be found than in "Interlude":

> Blow your tin squeals
> On your reedy whistle.

> How they come
> > dancing,
> White girls,
> > lithe girls,
> In linked dance
> From Attica.
>
> Gay girls dancing
> > in the frozen street,
> Hair streaming, and white raiment
> Flying,
> Red lips that first were
> Red in Ephesus.
>
> Gone!
> You? Red-nose, piping by the Red Lion,
> You!
> Did you bring them?
>
> Here, take my pennies,
> *'Mon semblable, mon frère!'*[43]   (CP, 50)

The image is as perfect as it is exquisite, and the poet has success-
fully transferred both the spirit and vividness of his "Greek dream"
to a contemporary scene. Indeed, it may be no exaggeration to say
that the dancing girls and red-nosed piper are more alive and picturesque than the god Pan and his nymphs, who have never had any
real existence apart from myth and art.

CHAPTER 3

The Soldier, Lover, and Exile

SOME of Aldington's early poems may be said to anticipate his *Images of War*, for they were obviously written after England entered the war in 1914 but before the poet enlisted in the army in 1916. In one of these early poems, "Sunsets," the reference to Flanders leaves no doubt about the events which are taking place:

> The white body of the evening
> Is torn into scarlet;
> Slashed and gouged and seared
> Into crimson,
> And hung ironically
> With garlands of mist.
>
> And the wind
> Blowing over London from Flanders
> Has a bitter taste.   (*CP*, 68)

Two other pieces are dated by their subtitles, even though their content makes it reasonably clear that a war is in progress. "Hampstead Heath: Easter Monday 1915" is a picture of a nation at war, full of the fear of an impending air raid by German bombers. The last stanza of "London: May 1915" is a melancholy comment on the destructiveness of modern warfare: "I am tormented,/ "Obsessed,/ Among all this beauty,/ With a vision of ruins,/ Of walls crumbling into clay" (*CP*, 51). Another poem, "Fantasy," is a contemplation of the durable and the evanescent, of the "Greek dream" and "the new reality" mentioned by McGreevy.[1] This poem depicts the ancient gods as being asleep and at peace; their repose is scarcely disturbed by the clamor and suffering of men engaged in a world war, for the affairs of mankind no longer concern them.

I Images of War

The "Proem" that serves as an introduction to *Images of War* (1919)[2] expresses the poet's desire to share the divine tranquillity which he attributes to the gods. He knows that such a wish is futile under the circumstances, but he hopes for a personal as well as a general peace when the conflict is over. His former happiness has been destroyed, and he yearns for some respite from the calamities which are taking place about him. In the other forty-two poems in *Images of War*, Aldington reflects his experiences as a soldier during the years 1916–1919. His service on the Western Front, in the trenches, and on the battlefields provided him with firsthand details concerning the horrors of modern warfare. Some of his poetic accounts of these are vivid and poignant enough to invite comparison with the work of other English war poets such as Wilfred Owen and Siegfried Sassoon. Aldington had cherished his no "romantic-heroic" notions about war since his university days when he had studied Walt Whitman's *Specimen Days* and *Drum Taps*, and he has acknowledged his debt to the American: "Whitman made me see the reality; and I believe he has the honour of being the only poet of the 19th century to tell the truth about war."[3] It is unlikely, however, that he met either of his two contemporaries, Owen and Sassoon, during the war, although he wrote a poem, "In Memory of Wilfred Owen,"[4] several years later as a tribute.

From the start, Aldington found army life repugnant to his own nature and temperament. He makes his feelings clear in "Bondage," where "I am so far from beauty/ That a yellow daisy seems to clutch my heart/ With eager searching petals" (*CP*, 76). In "Dawn," he is on a long march with other recruits. As they "trudge along wearily,/ Heavy with lack of sleep,/ Spiritless," he fancies that all share the same "unspoken prayer:/ 'God, end this black and aching anguish/ Soon, with vivid crimson agonies of death,/ End it in mist-pale sleep'" (*CP*, 78). It is easy to understand the poet's weariness, as well as his longing to be free and at rest again; but his prayer to end the misery with "agonies of death" sounds false and absurdly melodramatic, especially since Aldington apparently wrote the poem in England before he was sent to the front.

Some critics may also object to these poems, among others, as being sentimental—and it is true that a decade later Aldington recognized such emotional "weakness" in the semiautobiographical hero of his war novel, *Death of a Hero*. But Aldington was a very sensitive man with an infinitely greater capacity for expressing love and compassion than either anger or hatred. His heroic (if ultimately futile) struggle to keep his sensitivities intact is evident in the "images of war," many of which contain no direct reference to warfare. Constantly looking backward to his "Greek dream," he was trying desperately to preserve the memory of it despite uncongenial circumstances. There is an echo of the earlier poem "Choricos" in "The Lover," as the poet speaks of personified Death, who now resembles a Valkyrie. Death is a gentle maiden in "Choricos," but this one "will clutch me with fierce arms/ And stab me with a kiss like a wound/ That bleeds slowly" (*CP*, 79). In both poems, however, Death soothes the dying man and brings him peace and rest.

"Reverie" expresses the poet's desire to escape from reality, and he again finds solace in his dream. The opening lines present a description of the reality; then the real world vanishes; and, when the poet loses himself in sentimental daydreams about the girl he has left behind, several stanzas describe a quasi-mythical world of the dead. Unfortunately, the piece is not characterized by vivid imagery—a shortcoming of a number of poems in *Images of War*— and the poet's account of his existence after death is developed with general rather than specific details. A quiet "land of many flowers, . . . bright sunlight and cool shade" (*CP*, 100) does not evoke a definite scene, and the reader must use his own imagination to supply the particulars, such as the kinds of flowers and trees and the topographical features of the landscape. Much of the poem, moreover, is an abstract discussion of love and death that produces no images at all.

While Aldington could not entirely abandon his past or his dream upon exposure to the awful present, since doing so would have left him without moorings for his art (and possibly for his sanity), he was very much aware of the grim reality of war. He makes no attempt to escape the reality in "Machine Guns":

> Gold flashes in the dark,
> And on the road
> Each side, behind, in front of us,
> Gold sparks
> Where the fierce bullets strike the stones.

In a near shell-hole lies a wounded man,
The stretcher-bearers bending over him;
And at our feet
Cower shrinkingly against the ground
Dark shadowy forms of men.

Only we two stand upright;
All differences of life and character smoothed out
And nothing left
Save that one foolish tie of caste
That will not let us shrink.   (*CP*, 93)

As a soldier and officer, Aldington did not shrink from his responsibilities in the face of the enemy, nor did he avoid his responsibilities as a poet in such vivid descriptions of battle. The calm objectivity of the poem almost belies the poet's own fear of the deadly bullets which are flying about him, and there is something both pathetic and heroic in his refusal to seek cover because it is contrary to the sense of manly pride which has been conditioned in him by his early training in the English public school. There is no sentimentality in this poem. Only in the long dreary intervals in the trenches or behind the lines did he allow himself such self-indulgence.

"Bombardment" is equally objective, but the poet cannot avoid betraying his terror in a situation which is far more dreadful than the one described in the preceding poem. The destructiveness of heavy artillery fire and the helplessness of men under bombardment find effective expression:

Four days the earth was rent and torn
By bursting steel,
The houses fell about us;
Three nights we dared not sleep,
Sweating, and listening for the imminent crash
Which meant our death.

The fourth night every man,
Nerve-tortured, racked to exhaustion,
Slept, muttering and twitching,
While the shells crashed overhead.

> The fifth day there came a hush;
> We left our holes
> And looked above the wreckage of the earth
> To where the white clouds moved in silent lines
> Across the untroubled blue.   (CP, 105)

McGreevy praises this poem for its "slight but powerful statement of a circumstance of war which, because it has the precision of poetry and because it is devoid of all argument, is, if the cerebral, passionless, academic pacifist robots only understood poetry, . . . of more value as a repudiation of war than all their polite polemical versifying."[5] It should be added that the "powerful statement" of the piece is due, in part at least, to the use of biblical prose rhythms, a feature of some of Aldington's verse which has already been noted in an earlier poem, "At Mitylene." These rhythms are quite apparent when "Bombardment" is compared with such passages as the description of the Flood in the King James Version of the Old Testament, and they impart a tone of gravity and awe to the lines.

The sadness and gloom of the aftermath of barrage and bombardment are affectingly expressed in "Battlefield":

> The wind is piercing chill
> And blows fine grains of snow
> Over this shell-rent ground;
> Every house in sight
> Is smashed and desolate.
>
> But in this fruitless land,
> Thorny with wire
> And foul with rotting clothes and sacks,
> The crosses flourish—
> Ci-gît, ci-gît, ci-gît . . .
> "Ci-gît I soldat Allemand,
> *Priez pour lui.*"   (CP, 93)

Death tends to diminish the differences between men, and only the callous or the embittered can feel hatred for an anonymous and dead enemy soldier. The lines may remind the reader of Wilfred Owen's sentiments in "Strange Meeting" in which the poet, slain suddenly on the battlefield, encounters the soldier whom he had killed the day before and discovers that his dead enemy feels no rancor toward him—only deep regret for "the undone years" and "the pity of war."

Aldington's sorrow over the fruits of war is revealed again in "A Ruined House." Here he is concerned about the fate of an unknown family, whose suffering he can only guess as he contemplates the ruins of their lives. Their child may very well have been one of the children in "Three Little Girls." In his compassion for the innocent martyrs to the vicissitudes of war, Aldington seems to forget his allegiance to the principle of free verse by breaking into a pattern of regular meter, with alternating tetrameter and dimeter lines:

> Marianne, Madeline, Alys,
> Three little girls I used to see
> Two months ago,
> Three little girls with fathers killed
> And mothers lost,
> Three little girls with broken shoes
> And hard sharp coughs,
> Three little girls who sold us sweets
> Too near the shells,
> Three little girls with names of saints
> And angels' eyes,
> Three little girls, where are you now?
> Marianne, Madeline, Alys.   (*CP*, 94)

Both "Three Little Girls" and "April Lieder" have the rhythm and sentiments which might justify their inclusion in books of verse for children, for they contain a gaiety and tenderness which all but conceal the deeper tragedy. As examples of imagist poetry, however, they violate some of the most basic rules. Not only does the poet entirely disregard the principle of free verse ("April Lieder" has rhyme as well as regular meter), but he sacrifices precision and concentration in order to obtain a captivating lyric quality. Admirable as the two poems may be, they also depend upon "sonorous" repetition of words, phrases, and sounds (alliteration and assonance are important elements in both pieces) for their effect rather than upon selection of the "exact word."

Warfare in the trenches had its own peculiar miseries and horrors, and a number of Aldington's poems refer to his experiences in the underground fortifications. Physical hazards and discomforts combine to create a mental anguish which is especially well expressed in one poem, "In the Trenches." In it Aldington begins by rejecting the idea that men are destroyed in war by "fear," or by

weariness and loneliness. What really destroys them, apart from
physical injury and death, are the attritional effects of war upon
their minds and nerves:

> . . . each rush and crash
> Of mortar and shell,
> Each cruel bitter shriek of bullet
> That tears the wind like a blade,
> Each wound on the breast of earth,
> Of Demeter, our Mother,
> Wound us also,
> Sever and rend the fine fabric
> Of the wings of our frail souls,
> Scatter into dust the bright wings
> Of Psyche!   (*CP*, 82)

The last four lines of this passage constitute a particularly skillful
adaptation of classical myth to the circumstances of modern warfare.
The visual quality of the image is strengthened by the mention of
Psyche, which here alludes not only to the mind or soul of man but
also to the beautiful maiden who was immortalized by her love for
Cupid.

One knows from Aldington's autobiography that the man did not
recover from his war experiences for many years. From the war
poetry already quoted, it is known that the stress on his mind and
nerves must have been severe; but not until the penultimate poem
in the group does one observe a man who appears to be breaking
under the strain. Though Aldington never suffered complete collapse in either body or mind, "The Blood of the Young Men" is
evidence that his sanity may have been threatened at one time:

> Give us back the close veil of the senses
> Let us not see, ah, hide from us
> The red blood splashed upon the walls,
> The good red blood, the young, the lovely blood
> Trampled unseeingly by passing feet,
> Feet of the old men, feet of the cold cruel women,
> Feet of the careless children, endlessly passing. . . .
> . . . .
> O these pools and ponds of blood,
> Slowly dripped in, slowly brimming lakes.
> . . . .

> But we, we are alone, we are desolate,
> Thinning the blood of our brothers with weeping,
> . . . .
> Praying that our eyes may be blinded
> Lest we go mad in a world of scarlet,
> Dropping, oozing from the veins of our brothers. (*CP*, 119–21)

Such lines should be disquieting to the most complacent individuals. In his agony, however, Aldington does not lose control of himself as a poet[6] as he develops powerful images—dreadful as they may be. The influence of Whitman's *Drum Taps* is here, perhaps as never before in Aldington's poetry, but without Whitman's cheerful optimism.

Images of War is characterized by a great diversity of images, emotions, and forms of versification. The discussion of the poems has indicated that one piece may be realistic, that another may reflect the "Greek dream," and that still another may contain both elements. A particular poem in the group may be objective or sentimental, calm or impassioned in its tone, abstract or concrete in its statement. It may express love or hatred, love of life or longing for death. It may or may not present an image, use figurative language, or make direct reference to warfare. Finally, it may employ free verse or regular meter and rhyme. The only feature shared by the majority of the poems is the nature imagery, for the poet continues to speak of the beauty of flowers, trees, birds, green meadows, dewy grass, ripe fruits and berries, quiet pools and streams, white clouds and sunny blue skies, moon and stars at night. More than half of the pieces contain significant images expressing the natural beauty of the world, which the poet is unable to ignore despite calamity and his own suffering.

II Images of Desire

Images of Desire was published the same year (1919) as *Images of War*. The twenty-three pieces in this group are examples of Aldington's early attempts to write verse which C. P. Snow regards as "some of the best love-poetry in English."[7] In these poems, even more than before, Aldington frequently ignores his devotion to free verse, but he often creates good images. While Aldington takes particular delight in the physical beauty of women, the reader has already seen that his love for them is more profound than mere sensual craving and that it is almost Platonic at times. In *Images of Desire*, however, the poet emphasizes the pleasure, to the point of voluptuousness, of physical contact with female beauty, as in the poem "Her Mouth":

> Her mouth is a crushed flower
> That unpetals marvelously
> Beneath my lips.
> . . . .
> The crimson that dyes her lips
> Dyed mine, so close were our kisses;
> All day I felt its soft caress
> Making smooth my lips.   (*CP*, 131)

or in the first verse of "Epigrams":

> Your mouth is fragrant as an orange-grove
> In April, and your lips are hyacinths.
> Dark, dew-wet, folded, petalled hyacinths
> Which my tongue pierces like an amorous bee.   (*CP*, 127)

In "Daybreak," Aldington employs regular rhyme and meter, and Hughes observes that the poet's "passion awakens echoes of Swinburne."[8] The lines succeed very well in expressing intense desire:

> The naked pale limbs of the dawn lie sheathed
>   in dove-white folds of lawn
> But from one scarlet breast I see the cloudy
>   cover slowly drawn.
>
> Not all the blood of all our dead, the bright,
>   gay blood so gaily shed,
> Shines with so clear a glow as gleams your breast-
>   flower from our candid bed.
>
> Ah, bend above me, dear, and take my life breath
>   with your lips and break
> My body up as wheaten bread, and use my very
>   blood to slake
>
> Your parching sudden thirst of lust. Be cruel,
>   love, be fierce and thrust

> Your white teeth in my flesh and taste how
>   honey-sweet is amorous dust.
>
> Ah! slay me with your lips, ah! kill my body's
>   strength and spirit's will
> So that at dawn I need not go but lie between
>   your breast-flowers still.   (*CP*, 133)

Lips and breasts as flowers are recurrent images in the poems, and violence of passion mingled with tenderness is characteristic of the group as a whole. The images are vivid, the passions are strong, but they are so without any coarseness or vulgarity; they are carnal in nature but delicate in expression.

Since *Images of Desire* was published at the same time as *Images of War*, it is not surprising that some of the poems of the former refer directly to wartime love. In addition to brief allusions to war in such pieces as "Daybreak," there are other poems which are dedicated to the subject. "Before Parting" is one of these, and it begins: "Love, though the whole earth rock/ With the shattering roar of the guns' booming,/ Though I return once more to the battle,/ Give me, O love, your love for this last brief season." The poet continues:

> Kiss my lips with your mouth that is wet with wine,
> Wine that is only less keen than your lips are;
> Slip from under your fragile garments as a white rose
> Slips from under her leaves to the naked sunlight;
> Give to my eyes your straight young body,
> The limbs that embrace me, the breasts that caress me,
> Whisper to me the sudden words of yearning,
> The broken words that speak an infinite yearning. . . . (*CP*, 137)

It is easy to understand the desperateness and intensity of Aldington's passion, for he needed beautiful memories to which he could cling until his next leave, which, after all, might never come—a possibility that he expresses in "Prayer." Furthermore, a number of the poems reveal an angst which turns into utter despair and disillusionment in the novel, *Death of a Hero*, as will be seen later.

The first and last poems in *Images of Desire*, "Prelude" and "Epilogue," resemble sonnets in their sentiments, structure, de-

velopment, and iambic pentameter lines. "Epilogue" is a particularly fitting comment on the poems as a whole:

> Have I spoken too much or not enough of love?
> Who can tell?
>
> But we who do not drug ourselves with lies
> Know, with how deep a pathos, that we have
> Only the warmth and beauty of this life
> Before the blankness of the unending gloom.
> Here for a little while we see the sun
> And smell the grape-vines on the terraced hills,
> And sing and weep, fight, starve and feast, and love
> Lips and soft breasts too sweet for innocence.
> And in this little glow of mortal life—
> Faint as one candle in a large cold room—
> We know the clearest light is shed by love,
> That when we kiss with life-blood in our lips,
> Then we are nearest to the dreamed-of gods.   (CP, 148)

Aldington has hardly "spoken too much of love," and he has presented some lovely images. But now, in the safety and comfort of
civilian life, his mind appears to be once again at peace in this
expression of the *carpe diem* motif.

III   Exile and Other Poems

Hughes indicates that "the bitterness which the War brought" to
Aldington has "its first violent expression" in *Exile and Other Poems*
(1923). As he observes, the seventeen poems of "exile" are written
"chiefly in free verse and blank verse, . . . voicing the disillusionment and despair which besieged the poet in the postwar days,
when memories of horror were still fresh, and when it seemed
impossible to make a readjustment to life along the lines of peace."[9]
In fact, postwar England and its inhabitants are loathsome and repugnant to Aldington after his experiences at the front. In his despair, he invokes the artist, in "Rhapsody in a Third-class Carriage,"
to make use of the homely and everyday material of the world to
which he has returned:

> Sculptor! show Mars
> bloody in gas-lit abattoirs,
> Apollo organist of Saint Mary's,

> Venus of High Street, Athena,
> Worshipped at National schools.
> Painter! there are beets in allotments,
> embankments, coal-yards, villas, grease,
> interpret the music, orchestra,
> trams, trains, cars, hobnails, factories—
> O poet! chant them to the pianola,
> to the metronome in faultless verse. . . .   (*CP*, 165)

The poet also suffers great anguish of mind. In his autobiography, Aldington mentions that his "nervous malady and insomnia increased rather than diminished" during the weeks which followed his return to England and civilian life:[10] "Every night as I read or lay sleepless I heard the raucous shouts and whoops of drunken revellers, a strange disorderliness in the decorous West End. I am no enemy to rejoicings, but this debauchery over ten million graves seemed to me indecent. I saw nothing to rejoice about, having too many vivid recollections of endless desolation and rows upon rows of wooden crosses."[11] Aldington appears to have chosen sobriety to drunkenness as he faced his memories of the war—a resolution not easily sustained. During the day, he could forget by immersing himself in his work, but at night he could not sleep. If he did not read himself to sleep at dawn with Sir Walter Scott's novels, he had hideous waking nightmares, such as those in "Eumenides":

> Loos, that horrible night in Hart's crater,
> The damp cellars of Maroc,
> The frozen ghostly streets of Vermelles,
> The first night-long gas bombardment—
> . . . .
> That boot I kicked
> (It had a mouldy foot in it)
> The night K's head was smashed
> Like a rotten pear by a mortar.   (*CP*, 153)

Other poems are less morbid. For example, "To Those Who Played for Safety in Life" expresses a cynical attitude toward the idea that life is as bad as it could be:

> I also might have worn starched cuffs,
> Have gulped my morning meal in haste,

> Have clothed myself in dismal stuffs
> Which prove a sober City taste;
>
> I also might have rocked and craned
> In undergrounds for daily news,
> And watched my soul grow slowly stained
> To middle-class unsightly hues . . .
>
> I might have earned ten pounds a week!   (CP, 174)

The use of exact rhyme and meter in this poem seems to be a felicitous choice on Aldington's part: it adds a tartness to the lines which is very attractive. "Bones," too, is rather gay and carefree in spirit:

> Now when this coloured curious web
> Which hides my awkward bones from sight
> Unrolls, and when the thing that's I—
> A pinch of lighted dust that flashes—
> Has somehow suddenly gone out,
> What quaint adventures may there be
> For my unneeded skeleton?   (CP, 156)

Furthermore, "Bones" does not express a pious attitude toward death, as one can see by the last stanza:

> I leave to those superior minds
> Who make theology their care
> The task of settling whose shall be
> These much-used frameworks at the last;
> I rather see a wearier world
> Shed, aeons hence, its comely flesh
> To dance, a mournful skeleton,
> Sedately round a dingier sun.   (CP, 157)

It is not that the poet does not want to believe in a life beyond mortal existence—it is simply that he *can not*. In "Meditation," he is tormented by the thought that he will someday lose the woman he loves, for he cries out pathetically against such injustice: "I would kiss the feet of man or woman/ Who would prove to me your immortality" (CP, 158). This lack of belief in a better world to come may also account for the poet's feelings of guilt at having survived many of his comrades during the war, as shown by the concluding lines of another poem, "In the Palace Garden": "This happiness is not yours;/ It is stolen from other men./ Coward! You have shirked your fate" (*CP*, 160). Since he cannot believe in an existence after death, he feels compelled to make the most of his present life, seeking worthy objects and meaningful goals for his efforts.

But Aldington is harassed by doubts as to modern man's ability to accomplish anything of consequence. "At a Gate by the Way" voices his uncertainty: "The shadows we pursue may not be shadows,/ The dreams we live with may be more than dreams . . ./ All this I hope; but when the autumn comes,/ O friend, I am filled with musing and distrust,/ So poor my harvest to this golden wealth,/ So teased my spirit to this opulent peace" (*CP*, 164). Nevertheless, the poet gradually gains a measure of peace and satisfaction as he recalls his "boyish dream of Greek serenity."[12] "Freedom" is one of the later poems in the group—a piece which must have been written some years after those which express agony and uncertainty:

> At last, after many years, I am saturated
> With pity and agony and tears;
> At last I have reached indifference;
> Now I am almost free—
> A gold pellet of sunlight
> Dropped, curdling, into green water.
> . . . .
> Over harsh slopes the centaurs gallop
> With whistling manes, a rattle of hoofs;
> White shapes rustle the dew-dripping thickets,
> Slim fauns dance by the grass track.
> I have passed through hate and pity,
> Desire and anguish to this:
> I am myself,
> I am free.   (*CP*, 166)

The poet's freedom from the horrors of the past finally finds utterance in the lovely poem "Nightingale," a piece reminiscent of some of the best of his earliest "images." Part of the poem is quoted below:

> Your voice—
> Ah, chastest, coldest thing!

The brief shrill clang of ice on glass,
The note of fragile metal sharply struck,
The lapse of waters.
. . . .
So wild a song once rose
From the women of Artemis
In some cold hidden valley
Where trees sombrely ringed
A black lake and cold mist glided
As the first moonrays
Glittered through clouds.   (CP, 169)

Aldington has come full circle during the years between 1912 and 1923. He has forgotten his anguish and recalled his dream. His art has remained intact. He is now prepared to create poetry that is unblemished by the memories of war and that is also unimpeded by the rules of imagism.

CHAPTER 4

The Poet's Spiritual Progress

BETWEEN 1924 and 1937, Aldington published five long poems—*A Fool i' the Forest, A Dream in the Luxembourg, The Eaten Heart, Life Quest,* and *The Crystal World.* In his composition of these pieces, he continued to experiment with various poetic techniques, often employing different techniques in the same poem. As in the case of his earlier verse, his best long poems are those in which he most consistently produces vivid images. The five poems do not show the development of an original or characteristic mode of poetic expression, but they offer an account of the spiritual progress of a sensitive man of culture and intelligence. They embody, in a more compact form, many of the feelings and attitudes which are expressed in Aldington's novels, and they frequently deal with the institutions and prejudices of society in a satirical manner.

I A Fool i' the Forest

Aldington calls *A Fool i' the Forest* (1924) "a phantasmagoria," and he takes the title, of course, from the first line of the melancholy Jaques' account to the duke of his initial encounter with Touchstone, the court jester, in Shakespeare's *As You Like It:* "A fool! A fool! I met a fool i' the forest" (2. 7. 12). The poet explains the design of the work in a prefatory note:

The application of this phantasmagoria will be apparent when the symbolical nature of the three characters—'I', Mezzetin, the Conjuror—is explained.
The trio are one person split into three.
'I' is intended to be typical of a man of our own time, one who is by temperament more fitted for an art than a scientific civilisation. He is shown at a moment of crisis, and the phantasmagoria is the mirror of his mind's turmoil as he struggles to attain a harmony between himself and the exterior world.

Mezzetin comes from the *Commedia dell' Arte*. He symbolises here the imaginative faculties—art, youth, satire, irresponsible gaiety, liberty. He is one or several of these by turns and all together.

In a similar manner the Conjuror symbolises the intellectual faculties—age, science, righteous cant, solemnity, authority—which is why I make him so malicious.

Since the poem was first published in 1924, two years after the appearance of *The Waste Land* by T. S. Eliot, it is not surprising that critics were quick to point out Aldington's indebtedness to his colleague. Humbert Wolfe has remarked that Aldington "could only see life darkly in T. S. Eliot's looking glass," although his "half-glimpse was worth the whole of the Imagist philanderings with verse which was only free in the sense that a bolting horse is free."[1] If *A Fool i' the Forest* is indeed indebted to *The Waste Land*, it is difficult to identify the debt beyond broad general similarities. Both poems are an expression of "the theme of post-war disillusionment."[2] C. P. Snow's label for Aldington's poem—"a fantastic Rimbaud-like nightmare of the modern world"[3]—applies equally well to Eliot's piece. Both poets also have a similar style, and both use a "stream of consciousness" technique. In Hughes' words:

The whole poem has extraordinary pace, and a great variety of rhythms. The narrative passages are in unrimed verse, irregular, but hovering about the norm of a four-beat line. Interpolated are many snatches of song, some of them rimed and metrical—some of them satirically doggerel—others in unrimed cadence. Moods alternate swiftly, thought flashes and disappears, scenes shift as in a dream. . . . The time is the simultaneous past and present, for consciousness and memory are blended.[4]

These comments are almost as descriptive of *The Waste Land* as of *A Fool i' the Forest*.

In Aldington's poem, however, the identities of the three characters remain distinct, albeit they represent different views of Aldington's own temperament; but, in Eliot's poem the trio, while present, are commingled with a multitude of persons and are less distinguishable as separate facets of one being, even though "Tiresias, . . . a mere spectator and not indeed a 'character', is . . . the most important personage, . . . uniting all the rest."[5] Furthermore, although both poems are satirical commentaries on society that condemn "the venality, lies and pretense of the modern world"[6] and deal with a crisis in the life of the artist, Aldington appears to be very original in his selection of details and denouement and in his expression of feelings and attitudes. Thus, each poet, in his own way, exposes some of the follies of twentieth-century mankind by taking the reader on a phantasmagoric journey in quest of self-fulfillment and meaning in life.

Thomas McGreevy notes the influence of Shakespeare as well as Eliot in three early cantos of Aldington's poem. In the first canto, he says, "There is Lear-like bitterness . . . in the dismissal of Scaramouche, the professional court jester,"[7] and he quotes these lines: "I want a fool,/ A true, a bitter fool, who's looked at life/ And sees it's naught" (*CP*, 194). He also discerns "echoes from Ophelia's song"[8] in *Hamlet* (4. 5) in the elegy from the fourth canto of the poem: "*O tread upon the violet and the rose,/ Lay waste the hyacinths among the rocks;/ He will not come again*" (*CP*, 198). Finally, he observes that Aldington indicates in the seventh canto that he is familiar with Eliot's poems[9] (in this case, "The Boston Evening Transcript"):

> *O Evening Star,*
> *You bring the Evening News,*
> *You bring the tired business man*
> *Back to his tired spouse;*
> *Sappho and Shelley you no longer bring.*   (*CP*, 202)

Aldington's conception of *A Fool i' the Forest* appears to have its origin in the poems of "exile" which have been discussed. In his apostrophe, "Truth," he concludes by addressing Falsehood, whom he beseeches to "Make me a merry fool" (*CP*, 172). As his search for such a "fool" continues the length of the first canto of *A Fool i' the Forest*, he invokes a number of Zanni of the *Commedia dell' Arte*: "Send me a jester, send me Mezzetin,/ Brighella, Feste, Bagatino, Trivelin;/ No matter whom, but let him be a fool" (*CP*, 193).

The second canto recalls memories of the sights and sounds of Venice with fragments of Italian song, and ends by parodying *King Lear* and the first section of *The Waste Land:*

> Break, break, my heart,
> Flow down, my heavy tears,
> For Gargamelle is dead
> And all the world's too small to bury her.

> *'Twas Venice saw our true love's birth*
> *With soft Italian song and mirth,*
> *At Oberammergau—Herr Gott!—*
> *I loosed her tender virgin knot.*

Now lies she there. . . .   (*CP*, 196)

In the next line, the narrator has found his fool: "We three set sail for Athens,/ Mezzetin, the Conjuror and I" (*CP*, 196). The voyage is long and dull; the narrator becomes seasick; but the travelers at last arrive at their destination:

> I wanted to sit down beside the Parthenon
> And see the lizards on the broken steps,
> And hear the wind among the columns,
> Arcadian fluting, and look out to sea
> To watch for Theseus's sail.
> But the Conjuror was obdurate;
> He would keep talking of Thucydides
> And frightened me with all he knew of Pheidias;
> I couldn't interrupt because he'd paid our fares.
> Then he kept fanning with his bowler hat
> And spouted French. . . .   (*CP*, 197–98)

Throughout the poem, as Hughes observes, "The soul of the man is fought for by the poet and the scholar,"[10] by Mezzetin and the Conjuror, respectively. At the time of writing, Aldington was torn between the necessity of earning a living and the desire to leave England forever in quest of his early "Greek dream." This conflict, combined with the long hours required to complete his regular and contractual literary work, plus his composition of *A Fool i' the Forest*, had led to a brief psychosomatic illness. Thus, in the poem, the artist in Aldington yearns for the leisure to devote all his time to an appreciation of the beauty of the world; but the scholar in him, who is paying his way from the proceeds of criticism and translation of French literature, makes such demands on his time and attention that his truly creative talents are almost stifled.

The drowning "in the flood of moonlight" in the next canto is reminiscent of "Death by Water" in *The Waste Land*, and it is followed by the temporary rebirth of the poet and his "Greek of dream," which is accompanied by a change of mood.

> Mezzetin shook the moonlight from his strings
> And swayed and nodded as his fingers madly twitched;

> Swarms of silver wasps flew upwards
> With a buzzing of metallic wings,
> Here and there a crimson butterfly
> Rose and floated through the heavy air,
> Then swooped down and settled on my heart.   (*CP*, 203)

The trio are drunk on wine by this time; the Conjuror is half asleep; Mezzetin is softly strumming his mandolin; while the narrator is quietly contemplating Greek art. McGreevy states that the ensuing comparison of ancient Greece with contemporary England "is particularly significant because of the critical attitude it indicates on the part of Richard Aldington to Baudelairism and its post-war echoes in the more superficial . . . expressions of Mr. Eliot's talent."[11] He quotes these lines: "Yet this Parthenon is harmony./ Science and beauty reconciled with health./ We have beauty that's diseased and wanton,/ Art that plays with ugliness and fantasy,/ . . . / Our Parthenon's a Jew hotel" (*CP*, 206–207).

Mezzetin falls asleep, and the narrator has a vision of Hell, which turns out to be an industrialized Paradise where the values of commercialism are perpetuated by a God who is nothing more than an exalted baron of business and industry (an "everlasting Wanamaker," as D. H. Lawrence would say).[12] Aldington's irreverent burlesque of divinity underscores his contempt for a society which is obsessed with the continuous creation of artificial needs in order to provide a market for the increasing production of goods. This kind of civilization, from his point of view, destroys the truly creative spirit of man, along with the harmony of mind, body, and art. In addition, the passage contains references that reflect his disdain for organized sports, which were, in his opinion, also inimical to the development of this harmony with its accompanying artistic spirit and values.

At this point, Mezzetin awakens and rescues the narrator from Hell with "a coil of melody" (*CP*, 209), which is later followed by a fatuous ragtime song reminiscent of "that Shakespeherian Rag" in *The Waste Land:*[13]

> O Pall Athena
> Amurica lo-oves you,
> O Pall Athena
> Here's a han' to you-ou
> Hoodle-hoo, hoodle-hoo.
> Our biggest high-brows

> Are nuts on culture,
> An' our Co-eds are
> Readin' Homer through,
>   Toodle-oo, toodle-oo,
>   Our millionaires are buyin' Euri-pedes too
>   Hoodle-hoo, hoodle-hoo,
> And down in Boston where they bake the beans
> They know what Happapappazouglos means,
> So Pall Athena
> Here's a han' to you
>   Hoo-hoo-hoo-hoo.   (CP, 213)

Since Mezzetin's irreverence is more than the goddess herself can bear, she appears briefly before the trio in a menacing attitude; and they cower in terror at her presence. Then the Conjuror awakens, and the narrator argues with him "until the Greek dream has melted away."[14] Now the Parthenon disappears and the scene changes. The trio has found themselves in the long "dark ages" of European civilization, where Mezzetin symbolizes the mildness and stark beauty of the medieval church; the Conjuror, its harsher aspects—scholastic sterility, crusading zeal, and inquisitorial suppression. Finally, the scene changes again, and the trio are "beneath a sunny sky" (CP, 221) somewhere in France.

The nightmarish journey appears to have come to an end, but the Conjuror demands that the narrator select one or the other of his two companions or dismiss them both, warning him that it is impossible to reconcile the poet and the scholar whom they represent. Finding no escape from his dilemma, the narrator relinquishes the initiative to the Conjuror. Darkness has fallen once more, and they are at the front. The Conjuror, as sergeant-major, is in charge, and the other two are privates: "Off we went, to the music of night-firing,/ The pleasant evening hymn of Lewis guns/ And the pretty fire-works from the line" (CP, 228). The "music" turns out to be a dirge, anticipating the "symphony" of war—as Aldington himself describes it[15]—in the novel, Death of a Hero.

The Conjuror takes his companions on patrol; and, when Mezzetin becomes entangled in the barbed wire, he maliciously provokes enemy fire by shooting at a nonexistent German soldier: "Up went the Verey lights, down came minnies,/ Rifle-bombs, grenades, rifle-fire,/ And a beautiful scherzando of machine-guns./ Gradually the concert quieted down" (CP, 229). This passage is an expression, in briefer form, of the finale of the "symphony of war" which is later described in the concluding pages of *Death of a Hero*. Knowing that Mezzetin has been killed, the narrator realizes he has lost "something vital . . . for ever" (*CP*, 229) and is distraught with grief. The loss of "something vital" is the death of the poetic spirit and the "Greek dream," which Aldington had tried to keep alive throughout the war. This death represents everything that Mezzetin symbolizes—"art, youth, satire, irresponsible gaiety, liberty," all the "imaginative faculties" which are attributed to him in the author's note that explains the design of the poem.

The two survivors return to London, and the Conjuror drags his bored companion off to a continual round of nights at parties and of days at the British Museum. Following discharge from the army, Aldington found it difficult to readapt himself to the social milieu that he had enjoyed before the war. Furthermore, he committed himself to a life of scholarly toil which, although it paid well, failed to give him adequate satisfaction. As in the case of his narrator, neither the parties nor the work gratified him; he longed for the poetic spirit that had been slain within him. Like Aldington, the narrator is unable to sleep at night; and, as he walks the streets of London to calm himself, he thinks about matters: "Political assassination I rejected—/ Useless to cut off one Hydra-head;/ Anarchist attacks—futile and cruel;/ Bolshevism—a silly tyranny;/ Some inbred scepticism destroyed all my plans" (*CP*, 234). This passage is interesting because it reveals, in capsule form, Aldington's attitude toward politics. Even though he hated the British political system, he was unable to endorse the government of any other nation: his attacks upon capitalism are frequent and vehement; and his opposition to communism, while less common and more mild in comparison, is resolute and unwavering. His attitude may be best described, perhaps, as one of "noninvolvement," both in theory and in practice.

The Conjuror has plagued the narrator beyond endurance. One day, before dawn, as the two are standing on a bridge, the narrator hurls his companion into the Thames, "Down among the dead dogs and the Roman coins" (*CP*, 237). The dilemma is resolved. Lacking the power to reconcile the poet and the scholar, and incapable of choosing between them, the narrator has been forced to accept the only remaining alternative—he has lost them both. The outcome is inevitable:

> Every morning now at half-past seven
> Ethel thumps me on the back;

> Up I leap, a loyal English husband,
> —Whistle in the bathroom, gulp my bacon,
> Kiss the children—John and James and Mary;
> There's another coming, name not settled—
> Buy the morning paper as I hasten to the tube
> And read of all the wonders of the age.
>
> At the office I am diligent and punctual,
> Courteous, well-bred, and much respected;
> . . . .
> My will is made, my life's insured,
> The house is being slowly purchased;
> Yesterday I bought a family grave.   (*CP*, 237–38)

Earlier, in another poem, "To Those Who Played for Safety in Life,"
Aldington anticipates the lines quoted above; and later, in prose, he
describes the fate which he sought so desperately to avoid: "I should
be a fairly prosperous provincial lawyer, married to the daughter of
some local personage who could bring business my way. . . . In
politics I should invariably support the Conservative candidate. . . .
I should attend church regularly. . . . I should not read much
beyond journalism and detective stories. . . . Much of my leisure
would go to golf and tennis. . . . Occasionally I should invariably
express the original idea that there's no place like home."[16] Although Aldington's father or brother may have served as a model for
this description, it hardly represents a life of boredom and
mediocrity—much less so, for that matter, than the humdrum cleri-
cal career of the narrator in the poem. Not all men are suited by
temperament for the sort of vocation that Aldington chose to follow,
and he undoubtedly would have been miserable had he been compelled to serve as prime minister or archbishop of Canterbury, since
these men, like his father and his brother, were representatives of
the Establishment which he hated so fiercely. In reality, however,
he had to compromise. Though his allegiance was to the poet Mezzetin, Aldington prudently obeyed the Conjuror when it seemed
practical for him to do so.

II   A Dream in the Luxembourg

Some four years later (1928), Aldington found the leisure to write
another long poem, *A Dream in the Luxembourg* (1930). Dedicated
to "B," who has been identified as Brigit Patmore, this work cele-

brates the beginning of the poet's long love affair with her.[17] The poem "pleased" him personally: he "enjoyed writing it; it was long enough to make a book by itself; it was constructed; it broke all the rules for modern poetry by having a beginning, a middle, and an end and by being comprehensible"; and "It could not without injustice have the label of any school or clique pinned on it." Owing to the disapproval of his friends, however, none of whom found any merit in it, he refrained from publishing it for two years.[18]

The poem opens with a rather lengthy series of prefatory thoughts concerning the love of a man for a beautiful woman. Paris, in the month of June, is the setting for the poet's daydream; the sun is shining; he is sitting beneath a tree in the Luxembourg, gazing at a nearby fountain and the passersby. Then the scene changes, and the narrative begins on a cold and rainy day in England in early spring. The poet is seated at his desk, "writing a dull article," when a telegram arrives from the lady he loves asking him if he would care to meet her at an inn in a little French town by the sea:

> In an instant my mind was made up—
> For would I not go ten thousand miles
> Only to look at her and to watch her living?—
> So I took my pen and wrote:
> "Starting immediately shall wire you again from Paris
> My beautiful love I adore you."
> And the telegraph boy, who is friendly, said:
> "It'll cost a lot, sir, three pence a word, sir."
> And I said: "I don't care if it's a pound a word.
> Take it back at once, and telephone to the garage
> That I want a car here in half an hour."
>
> Then there was the inevitable scene
> Of making excuses and arrangements and packing;
> But my mind was working like a high-power engine
> And I made no mistakes,
> Even remembered to arrange for my letters,
> And gave my address, American Express, Paris. (*CP*, 247–48)

Apart from the arrangement of the lines on the page, there is nothing whatsoever to distinguish this poem from ordinary prose, either in choice of details, in manner of expression, or even in the trite and prosaic simile, "my mind was working like a high-power engine."

This style is substantially that of the entire narrative which constitutes more than two-thirds of the poem.

In an attempt to unify and poeticize the narrative, Aldington
provides some recurrent images. He refers to his love as a "wood-
nymph" (CP, 243, 244, 248, 249, 256, 257, 258, 263, 264, 270) with
hair like "crisp ilex leaves" (CP, 244, 248, 265), and he calls her his
"high-breasted, high-spirited lady of Provence" (CP, 257, 263, 267).
He also speaks of his "heart . . . pouring out tenderness and devotion and desire like the tall fountain in the Luxembourg" (CP, 261,
267, 270). Unfortunately, the "poetic" phrases and passages do not
really achieve their purpose, for they obtrude conspicuously in an
otherwise prosaic context and do not constitute organic elements in
the narrative. Since Aldington is a very capable storyteller, a capa-
bility discussed in its appropriate place, he would probably have
been more successful had he written the narrative as a short story
rather than as a poem. The nonnarrative sections, however, tend to
be quite acceptable as poetry. In the final canto, which returns
abruptly to the scene in the Luxembourg where the poet is daydreaming, the "dust" image is skillfully linked to the images of the
fountain and the Venetian glass as the poet produces a fourfold
mental picture of dust, which has a faintly biblical ring:

> At that moment the tall white fountain jet
> Fell from its height, crumbled like dust of water;
> Like dust of water it fell to a faint bubbling.
> Light faded from the Luxembourg
> As a heavy cloud from the north engulfed the sun,
> And a chill breeze ran over me.
> The dream was broken, fallen into dust
> Like the white fountain, like a Venetian glass
> When the poison is poured in it.
> I saw the horror and dreariness of the world
> Which they tell me is the real world—the world of dust.
> . . . .
> I stooped to the ground,
> And with my finger-tip
> Took a tiny pinch of dust
> And put it to my lips—
>
> It had a very bitter taste.   (CP, 273–74)

III   The Eaten Heart

The Eaten Heart (1929), a shorter poem, takes its title from the medieval legend of the Provençal troubadour Sir Guilhem de Cabestanh and his sweetheart Margarida, the wife of Sir Raimon Castel-Rosselhon (Roussillon). In the original, or source, story, Sir Guilhem falls in love with the wife of his friend, Sir Raimon. When the latter discovers his wife's infidelity, he slays Sir Guilhem, tears out his former friend's heart, and gives it to his cook with instructions to prepare a tasty dish of it for dinner. Pretending to have no appetite, Sir Raimon allows his wife to eat the heart before he informs her of its origin, whereupon the horrified lady takes her own life by leaping from a nearby balcony. Sir Raimon dies in prison, and the tomb of the two lovers becomes a shrine for the knights and ladies of the land.[19]

Aldington's poem does not recount the story, and he makes no direct reference to the legend until late in the poem when he mentions it as an afterthought. The piece is a sort of philosophical monologue, much of which would require little or no revision in order to convert it into a prose essay, since it is often very rhetorical without producing any images and since no image is as vivid or as detailed as some of those in *A Dream in the Luxembourg*. None of the lines, however, are as distinctly prosaic as the majority of those in the other poem; for the poet manages throughout to impart a sublime quality to his words despite the absence of good images. Furthermore, if some of the more prosaic passages were indeed written as prose, the result would be an indisputably elevated prose, which would not be the case with the other poem.

The opening lines of *The Eaten Heart* introduce the conflict in the poem:

> Under the reign of Mr. Bloom
> When the loud machines beat on our minds,
> We, that are children of despair,
> Who see or think we see so clearly
> Through Philoctetes' pain and Timon's rage
> How all hope's vain, all effort null;
> We that tremble between two worlds,
> Half regretting the old dead Europe,
>
> . . . .
> What do we know of love?   (*CP*, 277)

Choosing James Joyce's twentieth-century Ulysses, Leopold Bloom, as the contemporary representative of frustrated love, Aldington searches for the answer to such frustration among the tragic figures of Greek legend as they are portrayed in the classical drama— Phaedra in Euripides' *Hippolytus* and Philoctetes in Sophocles' play of that name. To fit his own theme, Aldington takes the liberty "to re-interpret" Sophocles' play "as an expression of human loneliness" (*CP*, 280). He says that "what is true of the tortured Philoctetes/ . . . / is universal, true today, true of ourselves" (*CP*, 281).

Throughout the poem, Aldington is tacitly concerned with a spiritual problem, and his "inner loneliness" (*CP*, 282) may be equated with spiritual emptiness. He admits that one "cannot put everything down to the war" or "to the machines" (*CP*, 284). In his quest for a solution to the problem of human loneliness, the poet arrives at the same answer which has been available to Christians through a study of the Scriptures. The only difference is that he is searching, like Diogenes, for the perfect soul who will never disappoint him. He describes this person as one whose mind and spirit are the exact complements of his own, and he denies the possibility that spiritual fulfillment may be found in a nature greater than his own. He probably has no choice, however, for he has no faith in God or immortality and is seeking a spiritual experience equivalent to the kind which is ordinarily sought through religion.

The legend of the eaten heart, then, provides an appropriate symbol for the poet's sentiments: "It shows perhaps how a woman devours a man's life,/ But it also shows how the man's gift of himself is total,/ And the manner of her death shows how her response is total":

> Then we see how a woman's vanity and a man's imprudence
> And the brutality of the world of men
> (Who always envy the happiness of others
> And hate nothing so much as the perfect communing of lovers)
> How these things bring a sudden and tragic ending
> Leaving no fate for both but death.
>
> We have lost or thrown away
> The power to live in this positive tragic intensity—
> For if life is not a tragedy it is nothing.   (*CP*, 285)

These lines contain an important theme which Aldington explores later in his novel, *All Men Are Enemies:* contrary to the popular adage, "all the world *hates* a lover." The lines also contain another paradox, that one must lose his life to save it. The words of Christ in Luke 9:24—"whosoever will lose his life for my sake, the same shall save it"—are easily understood, since the martyr has the promise of eternal happiness beyond the grave. The poet's lovers have no such promise; their reward lies in a brief all-consuming passion; therefore, they must choose between a long life of spiritual desolation and a short life of spiritual fulfillment. There is no question about the poet's choice: he would prefer to love and live with a fatal intensity than to submit himself to the inner loneliness which plagues his generation. But doubts remain; for, even if he fulfills his role, he has no assurance that his partner will not betray him.

IV Life Quest

The spiritual progress of the poet may be observed in the three foregoing poems. In *A Fool i' the Forest*, the narrator sacrifices poetry and scholarship for security and respectability, a choice which consigns him to a life of dull mediocrity. In *A Dream in the Luxembourg*, he refuses to allow his responsibilities to interfere with his freedom, and he finds happiness with the lady he loves. Unfortunately, she does not love him as he loves her; the affair lasts only a season; and it leaves the poet more lonely and bitter than before. In *The Eaten Heart*, in which he seeks an answer to the spiritual problem of inner loneliness, the only solution, he decides, is to merge his entire being—body, mind, and spirit—with that of another person, to the point that neither, without the other, is capable of independent existence.

Although Aldington published several novels and a number of short stories, he did not write another long poem for about six years. In *Life Quest* (1935), he returns to the stream-of-consciousness technique, to the image as a means of conveying his thoughts and feelings, to poetry in a genuine sense, and to his search for spiritual fulfillment. At the end of the last poem, he acknowledges the futility of achieving a perfect union with a woman in this life; but, since he cannot believe in the immortality of the spirit and in a better life to come, he has to set forth alone again in quest of temporal sublimity. His loneliness is apparent in the first lines:

Rain in the Pyrenees. . . .

Tonight they will dance till dawn at Biarritz
And the *milors* will see their fun is clean
Dancing among the gold-topped bottles
Euro-African and clean
Between the futile mountains and the silly sea.

These are the Koh-i-noor
The diamond point of living light
Cresting the shadowy pyramid of the dead.

Hail to Thee, Amon-Ra,
And Oom to Thee, O Bouddha.

Tonight it will be very lonely
In the woods of Roncesvalles,
There will be a sighing in the damp branches
A cold smell from the leafy ground
In the blackness of pilgrim shadows.

Listen, listen until hearing dies
For the echoes of the ivory horn,
Stare your eyes to stone
But you will not see . . .

. . . the living among the dead.

The life quest falters
And the ankh unlocks no door.   (*CP*, 307–308)

This passage sets the mood and direction of the poem as the poet
begins his search for an oasis of "life" in a wasteland of death. The
journey begins in southern France, continues into Spain, and ex-
tends to Italy, Egypt, and England. In his quest, the poet explores
the past as well as the present, ancient belief as well as contemporary philosophy and religion. The cosmopolitan character of his
travels recalls again *The Waste Land*, although the details are very
different and original.

As in Eliot's poem, the scenes evoke the dead. They also provide
a thread of thematic continuity with the preceding poem, *The Eaten
Heart*, which is also concerned with "old dead Europe." From the

deathly stillness of the Roncesvalles woods, the poet journeys to Irun, where he hears harsh voices in a street as "dark as death" (*CP*, 309). He continues along the northern Spanish coast:

> In the morning I walked in Santillana
> Under a sky crystal and cobalt
> Shot with the arrow heads of swifts,
> Santillana half-dead city of flies,
> Reeking of cow dung splashed on broken cobbles,
> Half-dead city—O florid heraldries
> Stonily boasting the pride of dead hidalgos.   (*CP*, 309)

To the poet, the hidalgos are as dead as the Stone Age men of Grimaldi who believed in vain that they could save the soul by painting the corpse with "red ochre/ That apes bright blood the life-giver" (*CP*, 310). These men are as dead as the ancient kings of Egypt, whose effigies of Osiris embellish tombs that their immortal ka "has never entered" (*CP*, 310). The spirits of all are as dead as their bodies: "The Ship of the Dead has never come to port,/ It never started" (*CP*, 311).

The poet has reached the same impasse that he has in his other poems. He yearns to believe in the immortality of the soul, for this would emancipate him from his obsession with the futility of mortal existence. He longs to worship a living God, but he is disillusioned by the presence of so many dead gods who have apparently passed away with the men who believed in them. Furthermore, science is no substitute for religion: "Shall we make new gods/ Of the sine and tensor/ And skate the outside edge/ Of the finite world?" (*CP*, 312). But, since science offers no comfort for the spirit, the poet resumes his quest. He turns from the coast and makes his way to the interior of Spain:

> Under the Guadarrama in the spring
> I heard the nightingales in the ragged park
> . . . .
> But shrieking jays silenced the nightingales
> And drunken reds came shouting from the futbol
> Tearing down blossoms and rooting up the flowers,
> And I never learned what the dead queens tried to say.
> But I think the Hapsburg queens were glad to die.
>   (*CP*, 313)

Even Spain, one of the last strongholds of "old Europe," is dead. Decaying remnants of the past linger in the shadows of the magnificent Escorial. The grandeur of the past is gone, and twentieth-century civilization is mean and ignoble by comparison. At this stage of his quest, the poet can feel only disgust for the world: "Must I love my fellow neighbors,/ Must I palpitate in sickly earnest/ For two thousand million spiteful apes?" (CP, 314). In addition, the present generation has been cheated by the selfishness of its predecessors: "Oh, distrust all Heroes and Saviours,/ Oh, beware of the life-hungry Ancestors/ Preying on us, wanting to live in us" (CP, 316). Mankind, moreover, may realize immortality, but only in a physical or intellectual sense—not in a spiritual way: "There come more flowers/ But never again that one bright flower/ Plucked by your love to lie in her breast" (CP, 316–17).

His quest so far a failure, the poet returns to England. At home, he sees even greater desolation than he found abroad; there appears to be no escape from a living death. He notes that "An Etruscan tomb is gayer than London streets":

> Sharp-lined and glinting
> The traffic clots go curdling
> Through the dark veins of the town
> In sharp mechanistic spasms
> Like the fierce bleeding of a great machine,
> Breaking the rhythm of our blood
> Until the soft swirl and lapse of Thames
> Alone seem unreal.
>
> Bombed and blackened
> Drab as the totem of a giant slum
> Thutmosis' obelisk expires.   (CP, 319–20)

The poet has reached the lowest depth of spiritual despair. Since he can sink no lower, the only direction is upward if he does not abandon his life quest. He goes forth again, this time to France, the one "spiritual home" which he has found during his lifetime. There, in the south, he begins to understand life, ironically, through his experiences with death:

> Below the crooked bridge at Brantôme
> The water of the Dronne runs clear and cold

> Past the old garden of the monks.
> . . . .
> Under an old willow I saw
> The body of a dead snake in the water.
> It was so dead, so utterly inert and dead,
> . . . .
> Like a piece of old bleached rope
> Swaying softly dead under the sun.   (*CP,* 321)

In the image of the snake, the poet recalls the sight of men killed in the war. But this memory is not all:

> I saw my own body lying white and helpless
> Belly turned to the sun
> Gently swaying in the water
> Under the sunlight where the snake lay
> With all the queer taut snake-life gone limp and lost.
>   (*CP,* 321–22)

He is unafraid, feeling instead "a great peace" at the sight:

> I saw that which was the snake
> And myself and those others
> Softly dissolve and drift with the stream
> Down to the Dordogne
> Down to the Gironde
> Down to the great rollers of the sea,
> And return as rain or cloud or air
> But never again as a crisp-gliding snake
> Rustling its way over dried grasses,
> Never again as a human soul
> Avid for much living. . . .   (*CP,* 322)

Spiritually strengthed by his vision, the traveler once more follows a southward course. He has not overcome his nostalgia for the past, but he seems less morbidly preoccupied with the death of old Europe than before. First he goes to Sicily:

> Near Syracuse a few flowers—
> On Mount Hybla a few stunted shrubs
> A remnant sweet with honey-blossom,
> All that was left of many acres

> Many lovely acres of dawn-pink blossom
> Hummed over by myriads of bees.   (*CP*, 323)

He leaves, unable to bear the sight of so much devastation of "beautiful and sacred" places: "Poor Persephone of an island/ Raped by all the thugs of Europe" *(CP,* 323). Sailing westward now, toward the Golden Isles, the poet arrives at last at the end of his journey— the Pillars of Hercules:

> I stood on the last mountains of Europe
> Gazing at the first mountains of Africa
> Across the little straits
> Where the puny liners crawled in whiffs of smoke,
> Ceuta a pinch of pearl dust at my feet.
>
> Far to the west the long slow heave
> Of the huge Atlantic, slow slow heave
> Like the enormous breathing of a god;
> Far to the east in shining sunlight
> Ripples upon ripples
> The innumerable laughter of the mid-earth sea.   (*CP*, 324)

This moment is one of revelation for the poet, and the spiritual quest which he describes in four long poems finally bears fruit. In a flash, the answer that he has been seeking so many years is revealed as he gazes upon the awesomely beautiful scene before him, and he is "swept speechless/ By a huge choking wave of life" (*CP*, 324).

Aldington has found the "life" which he has sought—not in the glories of the past; not in conventional religion; not in love for other human beings, for these have been subject to death and decay; but in the eternal verities of nature—"the real holy ones/ Sun Sea and Earth" (*CP*, 325). This revelation does not mean, however, that he has discovered Truth except in a relative sense, for the truth of poetry differs from that of science, and the poet and scientist do not observe nature from the same point of view. In his role as poet, Aldington portrays a moving scene and invites the reader to share his emotions and insights. Not every reader will join him in his worship of nature, since the poet does not seek forces or influences beyond the visible phenomena which his eyes behold; but all should feel a portion of the power and beauty conveyed in the description of the scene.

The final canto of the poem begins with an exhortation, reminiscent of biblical prophecy, which expresses a concern for the welfare of mankind: "Men and women/ Before it is too late/ Will you not draw back from greed and destruction/ Ere the earth becomes a cruel desert/ And the sea a sterile pollution/ And the sun black with anger against you?" (*CP*, 326). Like many an ancient prophet, however, the poet despairs of having his message heeded: "When I think of the world of men and women/. . . / I bow my head in my arms/ And lament destruction and greed" (*CP*, 326). If the poet has given up hope for his fellow man, he has not lost one particle of faith in the revelation which he has experienced:

> But in myself I feel exquisitely alive,
> Life flows through me,
> In a touch beyond prayer I ask
> That my life quest go on till I die,
> Oh, let the Sun still be mine
> And the undying Sea
> And the Holy Earth!   (*CP*, 327)

Although he regrets that all men and women cannot share in his discovery, he rejoices in his own salvation; he knows that his spiritual quest has been worthwhile.

C. P. Snow employs the phrase "full of life" to characterize Aldington's writings as a whole.[20] Though one may contend that the earlier poems, novels, and short stories are too preoccupied with failure and death to be considered "full of life," it must be remembered that Aldington never gives up hope, that he never ceases in his quest for life from the moment he first sets pen to paper, and that he has far too much vigor as a man and as a poet to suffer a premature death. Each of his first three long poems, like many of the shorter ones, ends with some kind of death—physical, mental, or spiritual—but the poet survives to continue his pursuit of life until he meets with success. Regardless of the outcome in each instance, the pursuit itself is always "full of life."

As Snow explains,

No one can read him for ten minutes without feeling a glow of power and vitality: a gusto both of the senses and of the mind: a natural, fluid ease with words: an impression of someone seeing things ten times more vividly, and being both hurt and delighted ten times more intensely, than most of us can

ever manage. . . . His passions, his delights and his suffering, come to us as
deeply and honestly as they did to himself. He is a man with an unusual
capacity for them all. That is why he can enrich us with moments unlike
those of anyone alive. That is why he can give us an intimation of experience
so deep and yet immediate that we shall not see the world with quite the
same eyes again.[21]

This appears to be overstated, for it is doubtful that every reader
will share the intensity of Snow's reaction. Nevertheless, Aldington
does impart a definite "glow of power and vitality" to his words, and
his thoughts and feelings do "come to us as . . . honestly as they did
to himself."

Life Quest, then, does not mark the beginning of "life" in Aldington's poetry but the moment when he becomes most aware of
the significance and beauty of life—when he is finally able to voice
his "credo"[22] (Snow's term). The "inner loneliness," or spiritual
emptiness, which plagued the poet in *The Eaten Heart* has vanished; and he feels refreshed and exalted in spirit by an overwhelming surge of what he calls "pure life" (*CP*, 325).

V   The Crystal World

The final long poem, *The Crystal World* (1937), represents additional development in the spiritual life of the poet. Snow regards it
as "the finest of all his writing,"[23] and the composition which "convinced many of what they had gradually been suspecting for some
time: that Aldington has written some of the best love-poetry in
English."[24] The poem is divided into twenty-two numbered pieces,
twenty-one of which are quite short in length, ranging from three to
thirty-two lines; the twenty-second is much longer, comprising
about half of the entire poem, and is subdivided into eleven numbered sections.

The first twenty-one pieces are organized in a loose chronological
order resembling a sort of plot. Some verses are sonnetlike in diction and sentiments, and they would be indistinguishable from the
earlier "images of desire" if placed among them. The poet is passionately in love with a young dark-haired beauty:

> Nile-lotus among women, dear flower of girls,
> Exquisite as a slender dark hibiscus,
> Take my head on your young breasts, beloved,

> Touch my cheek with your delicate hands
> And—break, O my heart, break with longing.   (*CP*, 343)

Since he is now able to share his discovery of "pure life" with another, his ecstasy is greater than it has ever been before: "this woman's soul/ Reached out to mine, and we seemed one/ And there was an end of all loneliness" (*CP*, 344). The title and theme of the poem are also explained: "Out of our love we have built a crystal refuge/ Unseen but very strong and ours,/ Only we can enter it and be safe./ We dwell at the very heart of life" (*CP*, 345).

Aldington has found a means of perpetuating and enjoying the fruits of his labor in *Life Quest*. His crystal world, moreover, is not built of the easily destructible glass from which he formed a brief refuge in *A Dream in the Luxembourg*. Nor is it subject to annihilation by death (which is its weakness in *The Eaten Heart*): "to die for you were too small a gift;/ I shall live for you" (*CP*, 345). The following passage suggests the nature of the crystal world:

> It is a world which has no battlefield,
> No factions and no bitter strife for power,
> And scarcely touches yours.
>
> . . . .
> Our world where dawn blooms like a cyclamen
> Over the wooded hills and whispering sea,
> With roses and the rustling of vine leaves
> And sun upon the sands and ancient towns
> And all the lovely things that men have made
> And all simplicity and truth and trust
> Set as our jewels in the gold of love!   (*CP*, 346)

Aldington's adjective, "crystal," describes his world very well: a world of glass in a sense, his glass is of superior hardness and quality. So radiantly clear as to be invisible, it is felt rather than seen, but is felt only by the poet and his lover. Others hardly touch their world; and, because it is invisible and finds its expression only in the feelings of its two inhabitants, no one about them is aware of its existence or of the difference in the lives therein. The lovers are, therefore, as spiritually remote from the rest of humanity and its cares as if they were actually on another planet. Furthermore, secrecy and privacy are essential to the happiness of the fortunate pair, because unfeeling people would seek to destroy the crystal world if its existence were betrayed to them—and this important theme Aldington pursues in some of his novels.

A few lines later, the lovers separate, driven in some unexplained way from their crystal refuge by the cruelty of the other world; and the anguish of the poet is as intense as his former joy. After he has experienced the bliss of the crystal world, life in the ordinary one is unbearable. The beauty of nature no longer pleases him, and all lovely things are a torment to him because they remind him of the woman he still loves. He especially regrets the child which he now fears will never be theirs as a tribute to their love. After much misery, however, the two lovers are reconciled, and his renewed joy is even more ecstatic than before.

The last half of the poem is an attempt, through a different poetic technique, to explain the significance of the first part. The poet begins by asking two unanswered questions: "What is poetry? And what is love?" (CP, 355). He then retells the story of his life with his beloved in their crystal world, this time by means of narrative and philosophical comment which closely approach the disinterested prose essay; and he has the tendency to be more intellectual and less emotional, more analytical and less "poetic." First he tries to determine the feelings which motivate the lover: "What he seeks is an ecstasy and a peace—/ The strange ecstasy of being together/ So that they create their 'crystal world'/ Which is only the common world made vivid;/ The deep peace of being at one" (CP, 358). Nevertheless, "there are obstacles" (CP, 359) which society manages, in one way or other, to place in the way of the happiness of the lovers.

Since the lovers will not accept anything less than their crystal world, they become as miserable as they were happy—more miserable than they would have been if they had compromised. Salvation for the two, then, can be found only in their mutual realization that they must swallow their pride and try to rebuild their crystal world. The parting of the two lovers was probably essential, however, to the continued existence of their crystal world, since it might have eventually crumbled anyway through sheer surfeit of pleasure:

> "Give us our world."
> It will not be given; you must make it.
> Only from the purity of extreme pain,
> Can you build the crystal world.   (CP, 366)

Snow says, "For anyone who wants to know Aldington's writing, this is the work with which to begin and end."[25] He may be right if he means that *The Crystal World* is the ultimate expression of the poet's development as an artist, for it reflects the variety of Aldington's technique and the progress of his thought. Throughout the five long poems, the poetic spirit of Mezzetin has been resurrected again and again, each time to greater glory, along with the scholarly spirit of the Conjuror; and the two spirits have gained at least some measure of reconciliation in the work of the writer. It is this kind of development and progress in a literary career that often determines the difference between greater and lesser poets. Though Aldington's verse may not be regarded as work of the first order, his best short and long poems—including *A Fool i' the Forest, Life Quest,* and *The Crystal World*—certainly deserve a place among the minor classics of the twentieth century.

CHAPTER 5

The Ironic Hero

IN 1929, Aldington began publishing a series of novels which satirized English society. Though there are satirical and autobiographical elements in his verse, one discovers in Aldington's prose fiction the most complete expression of his sentiments and ideals—his attitudes toward art and literature, nature and natural beauty, love and marriage, war and politics, religion and education. As in his long poems, he is concerned chiefly with human efforts to seek happiness and self-fulfillment. This quest is made in not only his famous war novel, *Death of a Hero,* but in his other satirical novels as well.

I Death of a Hero

In his preface, Aldington calls *Death of a Hero* (1929) "a threnody, a memorial in its ineffective way to a generation which hoped much, strove honestly, and suffered deeply" (*DH*, 8). To accomplish his purpose, he departs from the usual format of a novel. The book begins with a Prologue which would more accurately be termed an epilogue, since it reveals the plot and catastrophe. The author explains that he is imitating in this respect the practice of the Greek tragedian in order "to avoid any cheap effects of surprise . . . so that if anybody read on it would not be for the trivial purpose of finding out what happened, but because they were interested in what I had to say and the way I said it."[1] Aldington describes the technique of the novel as one which he developed in his long "jazz" poem, *A Fool i' the Forest* (*DH*, 7): the narrative simulates "the different movements of a symphony,"[2] and he introduces each of the four major parts with a musical direction to indicate changes in tempo as the story unfolds.

The Prologue is in *allegretto* time. The war is over, George Winterbourne (the hero) is dead, and the survivors are regaining the lively tempo of prewar days. Despite the lists of casualties which continue to appear in the newspapers, everyone is trying to forget as quickly and as decently as possible the agony of the past four years. Nonetheless, George has left behind him five chief mourners: his father, mother, wife, mistress, and last (and probably only) close friend, a fellow officer who tells the story of the hero's life and death. The Prologue gives a detailed description of their reactions to George's demise, but it is preceded by a metaphorical comment on death: "A life, they say, may be considered as a point of light which suddenly appears from nowhere, out of the blue. The point describes a luminous geometrical figure in space-time; and then just as suddenly disappears. . . . Well, it happens to us all; but our vanity is interested by the hope that the rather tangled and not very luminous track we made will continue to shine for a few people for a few years" (*DH*, 11)[3]. Such a hope is all too seldom fulfilled, and George's case is no exception.

George's mother and father are called "grotesques" by the author (*DH*, 22), but they are presented as typical specimens of their time and class in spite of such obvious exaggeration. Neither has the ability to accept the realities of life or war: the father seeks escape and comfort in passive religious piety; the mother, in active physical lovemaking. As the narrator points out, George's wife, Elizabeth, and his mistress, Fanny, are "not grotesques." They are "enlightened" young women of their generation who have been "educated" by the theories of Freud and Havelock Ellis in sexual matters (*DH*, 24). They fight over George in a halfhearted manner while he is in the army, but both are interested in other men; they really do not care too much about George; and all three women—the mother, Elizabeth, and Fanny—manage to forget George quite quickly when they learn of his death.

The Prologue concludes with a brief account of the narrator's encounters with George. From a military standpoint, George's death was unnecessary, for the Germans were in retreat, and he was the only officer in his unit who was killed in the engagement. The narrator makes it clear that the word "hero" has only an ironic meaning in the book: "The death of a hero! What mockery, what bloody cant! What sickening putrid cant! George's death is a symbol to me of the whole sickening bloody waste of it, the damnable stupid waste and torture of it" (*DH*, 35). He asks the question: "How can we atone for the lost millions and millions of years of life, how atone for those lakes and seas of blood?" (DH, 35). Earlier, in a war poem, "The Blood of the Young Men," Aldington implies that adequate atonement is impossible in such a case. His narrator in the novel agrees, but he tries to find a way that is more meaningful than that of the others: "Headstones and wreaths and memorials and speeches and the Cenotaph—no, no, it has got to be something *in* us. . . . That is why I am writing the life of George Winterbourne, a unit, one human body murdered, but to me a symbol. It is an atonement, a desperate effort to wipe off the blood-guiltiness" (DH, 35–36). The rest of the book deals with the details of George's life from the circumstances surrounding his birth to the precise moment of his death, for the author attempts to establish a cause and effect relationship in the intervening episodes between the two events.

In Part 1, written in *vivace* time, the story of George's childhood is also an indictment of Victorian England, the smug, self-complacent England of 1837–1914; for, as the author explains later in the book, "the Victorians were still in full blast in 1914, and had pretty much the control of everything" (DH, 223). Through direct satire—commentary and treatment of characters—Aldington indicates that the Victorians, who are represented in the novel by George's parents and grandparents, were responsible for the war and for the slaughter of the young men of his generation. The first chapter opens on an almost Dickensian note: "A very different England, that of 1890, and yet curiously the same. In some ways so fabulous, so remote from us; in others so near, terrifyingly near and like us. An England morally buried in great foggy wrappings of hypocrisy and prosperity and cheapness" (DH, 39).

Lest the reader be lulled by this sentimental tune, the narrator suddenly strikes a brief discordant note, giving forth in the manner of an Elizabethan tragic hero: "Rummy old England. Pox on you, you old bitch, you've made worms' meat of us. (We've made worms' meat of ourselves.) But still, let me look back upon thee. Timon knew thee" (DH, 39–40). The account of George's parentage continues in this vein, and one cannot avoid remarking the influence of Charles Dickens in the tone, style, and use of caricature. But there are conspicuous differences in the writing of the two authors; for where Dickens expresses a genuine affection for his unfortunate characters, Aldington is ironic when, for example, he refers to the grandparents as "dear Mamma" and "dear Papa" or to the parents as "dear George Augustus" and "sweet Isabel" and is without sentiment in portraying them as contemptible creatures. He also spices his narrative with words and references which would have been unprintable in Dickens' time. As a matter of fact, many passages of the novel were unprintable in Aldington's own time and an unexpurgated edition did not appear until 1965. The censored passages range in nature from the four-letter obscenities that are most prevalent in the speech of common soldiers to such indelicate phrases as the following: "Prehistoric beasts, like the ichthyosaurus and Queen Victoria, have laired and copulated and brought forth" (*DH*, 118).[4]

Death of a Hero is obviously autobiographical to a very large degree, for George Winterbourne may be readily identified with Aldington himself on the basis of factual information supplied later in the author's autobiography and in various sketches by those who knew him. Like other "autobiographical novels," however, it is dangerous to assume parallels with the author's own life where actual evidence does not exist to justify them. The book should probably be regarded, therefore, as an artistic work of fiction in which the writer skillfully selects certain details from personal experience and alters others to create a coherent story with a theme. The fact that Aldington makes George a painter instead of a poet should be ample indication of the author's desire to de-emphasize the autobiographical aspect of the novel as much as possible, even though he appears to forget his purpose now and then by including irrelevant details from his own life. An example of this forgetfulness is the passage where George is credited with reading the work of the majority of English poets by the time he is sixteen (*DH*, 82)[5]—a rather difficult and incongruous accomplishment for a boy who finds it "so much more fun to paint things than even to read what Keats and Shakespeare thought about them" (*DH*, 77).

For the most part, George's youthful tastes and propensities are the kind which one would expect to be shared by persons of artistic temperament, by painter and poet alike: his love of nature and natural beauty, his hatred for organized sports and military drill, his preference for solitude and daydreaming, his predilection for the ideal rather than for the practical. The author does well to rely heavily upon the experiences of his own childhood, while artfully concealing the names of actual persons and places. Like Aldington, George Winterbourne spends much of his early life in the South Foreland area near Dover, where his emotions are first awakened to the beauty of the world about him:

The storm had blown itself out. . . . The heavy, dank smell of wet earth-mould came up to him with its stifling hyacinth-like quality, the rain-drenched privet was almost over-sweet; the young poplar leaves twinkled and trembled in the last gusts, shaking down rapid chains of diamonds. . . . The sun moved majestically and imperceptibly downwards in a widening pool of gold, which faded, as the great ball vanished, into pure, clear, hard green and blue. One, two, a dozen blackbirds and linnets and thrushes were singing; and as the light faded they dwindled to one blackbird tune of exquisite melancholy and purity. (DH, 73–74)

George is bullied by his schoolmasters because he rebels against their efforts to turn him into "a thoroughly manly fellow" (DH, 79), through sports and drill, "to conform to their minor-gentry, kicked-backside-of-the-Empire code" (DH 83). His attitude reflects the author's own feelings, for, as C. P. Snow observes, "the ordinary public-school young man is a symbol of everything Aldington most detests."[6] George is "really happy" only during summer vacation (DH, 84) when he is free to roam the countryside, sketch, paint, and read. He has few close friends—an amateur biologist who interests him in natural history, a middle-aged gentleman who introduces him to French literature and European culture, and a young lawyer who initiates him in the pleasures of long hikes through rural England—and all drawn from real individuals whom the author had known in his boyhood. At this time, George also becomes aware of the charms of the other sex. Aside from his boredom at the public schools, George leads a rather carefree and idyllic existence in rural Kent, much as the author had done; but his tranquillity and hopes for the future are suddenly shattered, as Aldington's were, by his father's financial losses through unwise speculation. Unable to pursue his chosen career and unwilling to accept anything less, he quarrels with his parents and departs for London to follow his own destiny.

The second part of the novel relates, in *andante cantabile* tempo, the course of George's life for the four or five years which precede his enlistment in the army. The hero's initiation into artistic and literary circles permits the narrator to comment on the intellectual milieu of London in 1912: "In the course of his *naïf* peregrinations George became temporarily acquainted with numerous personages, whom he classified as morons, abject morons, and queer-Dicks. The abject morons were those editors and journalists who sincerely believed in the imbecilities they perpetrated. . . . The morons were those who knew better but pretended not to. . . . The queer-Dicks were more or less honest cranks, or at least possessed so much vanity and obstinacy that they seemed honest" *(DH,* 110). Although the autobiographical nature of the book should not be overemphasized, the reader can hardly fail to recognize the "queer-Dicks," as well as a number of the unlabeled personages in the portrayals which follow. They are some of the most eminent men of letters of the twentieth century who are thinly disguised by caricature of incidental traits of their personalities.

Waldo Tubbe—with his Midwestern United States origin, his "Americanized Toryism" *(DH,* 110–11) and his "neat, mincing English," punctuated with exclamations of "Oe-oh," "Indeed," and "Really" *(DH,* 127–28)—is obviously T. S. Eliot.[7] To make certain that the reader will not err in the identity, Aldington attributes to Tubbe a garbled version of Eliot's famous creed. In his preface to a collection of essays, *For Lancelot Andrewes* (1928), Eliot states that his "general point of view . . . might be described as classicist in literature, royalist in politics, and anglo-catholic in religion"; and this summation reemerges in Tubbe's case in the nonsensical form of "Royalism in Art, Authority in Politics, and Classicism in Religion" *(DH,* 110)—a clue perhaps to Aldington's attitude toward many of the great writer's pronouncements.

By the same token, "Comrade" Bobbe, "a sandy-haired, narrow-chested little man with spiteful blue eyes and a malevolent class-hatred" *(DH,* 124), cannot be anyone other than D. H. Lawrence.[8] His resemblance to Lawrence is also borne out by "his working-class origin and his indigestion, of which he had been dying for twenty years" (Lawrence was dying slowly of tuberculosis), as well as by his "feverish energy," his "faculty of imitation," his "remarkable intuition into character," his "sharp tongue and brutal frankness," his desire "for affairs with upper-class women," and his description by the author as a "homosexual type" *(DH,* 124–25). All these characteristics are mentioned elsewhere by Aldington and other writers. As if this is not enough, Bobbe is also credited with "fatuous theories of the Unconscious, which were a singular mixture of misapprehended theosophy and ill-digested Freud" *(DH,* 125); and Bobbe himself speaks of an "out-reaching of the inward, unconscious Male-life to the dark Womb-life in Woman" *(DH,* 127)—a distinct reference to one of Lawrence's principles.

Shobbe, the editor of an English literary review *(DH,* 110), is certainly Ford Madox Ford. Called "fat Shobbe" *(DH,* 119) by his acquaintances, he is depicted in the following manner: "He was a plump and talented snob of German origin. . . . Before the Great War he was always talking about his year's service in an aristocratic German regiment . . . or saying 'Of course, you English. . . .' After the war he discovered he was and always had been a patriotic English gentleman. . . . After the comfort of his own person he really cared for nothing but his prose style and literary reputation. He was also an amazing and very amusing liar—a sort of literary Falstaff" (DH, 130–31). If the reader entertains any doubt concerning Shobbe's real-life counterpart, he needs only to refer to Aldington's description of Ford in Life for Life's Sake.[9] Mrs. Shobbe is probably Ford's second wife, Violet Hunt.[10]

Aldington's treatment of Eliot, Lawrence, and Ford is hardly flattering, but one should not expect anything else in a book designed as a general assault upon English society. Despite the classification of the three as "queer-Dicks," they are the most illustrious of George's London acquaintances, and the author tends to ridicule their personal foibles rather than their literary accomplishments. The author's real feelings toward these men, moreover, are somewhat twisted or concealed in the novel; for, as he treats them with genuine respect and affection in his autobiography, he acknowledges their virtues and talents as well as their faults and weaknesses.

It does not seem worthwhile here to attempt to establish the identities of all of Goerge's acquaintances, but three others deserve brief discussion—Upjohn, Elizabeth, and Fanny. Frank Upjohn, George's closest friend in London in 1912, is apparently Ezra Pound; but Upjohn is a painter instead of a poet: "Since he was destitute of any intrinsic and spontaneous originality, he strove much to be original, and invented a new school of painting every season. . . . At this moment he was just about to launch the Suprematist movement in painting, to which he hoped to convert George, or at any rate to get him to write an article about it. Suprematist painting, which has now unfortunately gone out of fashion, was, as its name implies, the supreme point of modern art" (DH, 112–13). Aldington no doubt is alluding to Pound's flair for starting new movements in poetry, in this case imagism, although Upjohn possesses other traits which Aldington has ascribed to Pound.[11] Among these are his conceit and patronizing attitude, his fondness for the term le mouvement (DH, 119), his habit of introducing spoken statements with "What I mean to say is" (DH, 113), his profanity, and his "furious onslaughts on any one who was established and successful, in alleged defence of any one who was struggling and neglected" (*DH*, 126).

Elizabeth and Fanny, however, cannot be readily associated with actual persons, though their physical appearance and personalities are described in considerable detail. Elizabeth, with her dark "Egyptian" features (*DH*, 132), resembles Aldington's mistress, Dorothy Yorke,[12] somewhat more than she does his wife, Hilda Doolittle. Fanny, with her blonde hair and "gem-like" eyes (*DH*, 178), faintly resembles Hilda.[13] Similarities of personality are even more difficult to ascertain, and it would serve no purpose to pursue the matter further. On the other hand, the two women in the novel are too complex and lifelike to be dismissed as mere caricatures, although they seem a bit eccentric in their espousal of "advanced" attitudes toward sexual behavior which are more characteristic of the postwar generation.

The author brings all these characters, except Fanny, together at a typical social gathering of artists and writers where the conversation abounds in "witticisms" and petty gossip rather than in any serious exchange of ideas. At this meeting, George meets Elizabeth; and the remainder of Part 2 of *Death of a Hero* is an exploration of George's relationship with the two women during the next few years. George's relationship, already outlined in the Prologue, is now developed in detail and dialogue, so that the reader is able to follow the chain of circumstances leading to the hero's destruction.

This part of the novel is not pure narrative, for it contains much commentary on the state of society at the time. The author makes it clear that the two women should not be held responsible for the hero's death. He maintains that the real villains were George's elders, as well as the parents and the grandparents of all the young men who died in the war:

I have shown, with a certain amount of excusable ferocity, how devilishly and perniciously the old régime of Cant affected people's sexual lives, and hence the whole of their lives and characters and those of their children. . . . It was the régime of Cant *before* the War which made the Cant *during* the War so damnably possible and easy. On our coming of age the Victorians generously handed us a charming little cheque for fifty guineas—fifty-one months of hell, and the results. . . . But it wasn't their fault? They didn't make the war? It was Prussia and Prussian militarism? . . . Who made Prussia a great power and subsidized Frederick

the Second to do it, thereby snatching an empire from France? England.
Who backed up Prussia against Austria, and Bismarck against Napoleon III?
England. And whose Cant governed England in the nineteenth century?
But never mind this domestic squabble of mine—put it that I mean the
"Victorians" of all nations. (*DH*, 221–22)

Critics have sometimes characterized Aldington's work as being
"bitter," and this passage, along with others in the book, could seem
to justify this adjective in describing *Death of a Hero*. As Snow
warns the reader, however, the word should not be employed indis-
criminately or without some qualification: "The bitterness is there
all right. But it only predominates in one or two books, and in them
is accompanied by much else."[14] He adds: "[Aldington] saw his own
generation led through collective stupidity into one war, and the
generation after it being prepared for another. . . . It is the opposite of his ideal. . . . He has met it with satire, anger, and brutal
shockingness. . . . In doing so, he has produced this impression of
bitterness of which we hear so much."[15]

Aldington's honesty, then, compels him to write the way he does.
He seeks the beauty of the world about him, but he sees its ugliness
at the same time.[16] For example, when George and Elizabeth are
gazing in "absorbed delight" at the "silvery water" of the Thames
and at the "moon-washed outlines of the city," they suddenly become aware that "on every bench sat crouched or huddled one or
more miserable, ragged human beings" (*DH*, 185). The proclivity of
the Victorian middle classes for neglecting and destroying beauty is
the subject of some of his earliest poems, such as "Childhood" and
"Eros and Psyche," but it is a recurrent theme in his later work as
well. In Part 1 of the novel, British philistinism effectively prevents
George's father from becoming an aesthete and a writer, and it very
nearly aborts the painting career of the son. In the end, of course,
the philistines triumph, for the hero's career is prematurely terminated by the war which their "Cant" has created.

Although George's difficulties with Elizabeth and Fanny prompt
him to enlist, he could not have avoided induction into the army.
While "he did not believe in the alleged causes for which the War
was fought" and "could not take part in the War with any enthusiasm or conviction," he also "saw the intolerable egotism of
setting up oneself as a notable exception or courting a facile martyr-
dom of *rouspétance*" (*DH*, 224). This attitude is expressive of the
author's own sentiments concerning the war.[17] Upon enlisting,

however, George finds that he is far unhappier than he was before, for "the suffering which was common to all decent men and women was increased and complicated and rendered more torturing by his personal problems, which somehow became related to the War" (*DH*, 224). It is only a question of time before his misery becomes intolerable.

As has already been indicated, the first two parts of the novel contain many references to Aldington's own feelings, ideas, interests, and experiences; he even recalls not only his "Greek dream" as he traces George's wanderings as a child through the lovely unspoiled English countryside but also his passion for flowers as he takes George and Elizabeth on a tour of Hampton Court. The same is true of Part 3—the "war" section of the book—for, as the author states in his autobiography, "Everything or almost everything I have to say about the war of 1914–18 has been said in *Death of a Hero* and *Roads to Glory*."[18] It may be assumed, then, that this part of the book is a fictionalized account of his actual experiences in the war, although little documentary evidence supports such accounts in his novel, stories, and poems.

Part 3 is in *adagio* time. Although this section is the longest and slowest movement of the four-part "symphony" in prose, it is also the most stirring. If George's life drags wearily from camp to camp and through the trenches and across the battlefields, the reader's attention does not share the same fatigue. Indeed, the hero's childhood in Kent and his young adulthood in London are relatively dull by comparison, for the author often fills the pages with social criticism and philosophical commentary at the expense of narrative and dialogue. At the front, George's experiences form a series of events that become progressively more painful and horrifying as time passes. When he suffers acutely from unanticipated humiliations, those among the worst are the dirt, the filthy water, the persistent diarrhea, the boils and the lice which infest his body. In addition, horror of the "well-fed rats" (*DH*, 280) which swarm about the trenches becomes an unforgettable aspect of the war which also finds expression in the author's poetry. Even worse, the hero becomes aware that "his mind degenerated; slowly at first, then more and more rapidly" (*DH*, 288). He discovers with "horror" that, under the rigors of army life and routine, he is "less and less able to enjoy subtleties of beauty and anything intellectually abstruse" (*DH*, 288). This blow strikes at his very "soul," so to speak.

The culminating event in George's experiences at the front is a battle that begins with a bombardment which is far more dreadful than any of the previous ones. One night, in the cellar of the ruined house where he is billeted, more than a mile behind the front line, George is startled from a deep slumber by a tumultuous din that exceeds anything he believed possible: "The whole thing was indescribable—a terrific spectacle, a stupendous symphony of sound. . . . The roar of the guns was beyond clamour—it was an immense rhythmic harmony, a super-jazz of tremendous drums, a ride of the Walkyrie played by three thousand cannon. The intense rattle of the machine-guns played a minor motif of terror. . . . The colossal harmony seemed to roar louder as the drum-fire lifted from the Front line to the Reserve" (*DH*, 321). Although elements of this "symphony" in terror may be found in the author's war poems and in a passage in *A Fool i' the Forest*, it is only in the context of the novel that Aldington manages to convey the full impact of the situation—to play, so to speak, more than a few bars of the melody.

The battle constitutes the highest point of dramatic tension in the symphony of George's life. The climax of the story, it is the beginning of the end for the hero. Battered in body and mind by the concussions of exploding shells and flying debris, unnerved by the blood and shrieks of wounded and dying men, and weakened by ague and pleurisy, he has reached that stage of battle fatigue from which Aldington himself did not recover for many years. George, however, suffers most from loneliness, from lack of companionship with men who share his tastes and interests. He cannot even anticipate any real comfort by becoming an officer, which is indicated by his acquaintance with Lieutenant Evans, his platoon commander: "Evans was the usual English public-school boy, amazingly ignorant, amazingly inhibited. . . . He accepted and obeyed every English middle-class prejudice and taboo. . . . He was exasperatingly stupid. . . . He could be implicitly relied upon to lead a hopeless attack and to maintain a desperate defence to the very end. There were thousands and tens of thousands like him" (*DH*, 285–86).

The "Public School fag" or "adult Boy Scout" is caricatured in the Prologue in the person of Sam Browne, a young officer on home service who has the distinction of being George's mother's twenty-second lover (*DH*, 18). This type of man both George Winterbourne and Richard Aldington hate most; he is the sort of human robot which they have struggled so desperately not to become themselves, despite the pressures of their parents, friends, schoolmasters, social class, and country. It is also significant that they do not hate individual men but only the mentality and values of such men as Evans and Browne. *Death of a Hero* is a "memorial," as Aldington points out, to an entire generation of young men of all classes and backgrounds (*DH*, 8), a memorial to Winterbourne and Evans alike, who, along with a million others, were forced to suffer for the stupidity of their fathers and forefathers.

Perhaps one now has an explanation for George's reluctance to accept a commission. In terms of tastes and interests, he has little in common with most of the men whom he meets in the army, either the lower-class Tommies or the middle-class officers; but he appears to feel that the first pose less of a threat to his ideals than the men of his own class. The noncommissioned Tommy officers may harass and humiliate George as much as they please, the other Tommies may ridicule and persecute him for being different, but the gulf between his class and theirs is too wide for them to touch his inner being. In describing the hero's relations with these men, moreover, the author skillfully recaptures their homespun humor and artless amiability; and these qualities are conveyed to the reader in a variety of dialects that are frequently punctuated with the four-letter obscenity familiar to all English-speaking peoples.

When George finally returns to England for training as an officer, he discovers that he is unable to readjust to the life which he had given up when he joined the army. His wife, mistress, and other former acquaintances bore him; and they in turn find him very dull company—he cannot communicate his thoughts and feelings to persons who have not shared his recent experiences. After a few months in England, he finds himself in the same French village where he had been billeted before. The village has suffered even more destruction and the nearby cemetery is much larger. He is put in charge of a company of young, inexperienced recruits; and, to make matters worse, the battalion commander is a former training-camp corporal who harasses his men to the limit of their endurance. The lack of necessity for such harassment in the line is indicated by the relaxed discipline of the first-rate Canadian troops whom George and his men are replacing in the trenches.

As the narrator observes, George takes his misfortunes "far too tragically and responsibly" during the months that pass; he broods constantly and sees "all things in terms of the bleakest despair" (*DH*,

365–66). An unusually sensitive man in an unusually trying situation, George moves "through impressions like a man hallucinated"
(*DH*, 366) and sees only death about him:

At dawn one morning when it was misty he walked over the top of Hill
91. . . . The ground was a desert of shell-holes and torn rusty wire, and
everywhere lay skeletons in steel helmets, still clothed in the rags of sodden
khaki and field grey. Here a fleshless hand still clutched a broken rusty rifle;
there a gaping, decaying boot showed the thin, knotty foot-bones.
. . . Alone in the white curling mist, drifting slowly past like wraiths of the
slain, with the far-off thunder of drum-fire beating the air, Winterbourne
stood in frozen silence and contemplated the last achievements of civilized
men. (*DH*, 366–67)

These are some of the nightmarish images that sear the hero's brain,
new horrors which are added to the repetition of old ones—lice,
rats, trench-foot, snipers, raids, mortar attack, machine-gun fire,
gas barrage, artillery bombardment and drumfire—and which are
complicated further by physical shock, exhaustion, and illness since
George is again plagued by the continual fits of chills and fever that
had weakened him before. His despair, moreover, is intensified by
the memory of a speech delivered to the new officers upon their
arrival at the front: " 'You are the War generation. You were born to
fight this War, and it's got to be won—we're determined you shall
win it. So far as you are concerned as individuals, it doesn't matter a
tinker's damn whether you are killed or not. Most probably you will
be killed, most of you. So make up your minds to it' " (*DH*, 227). It
is therefore no real consolation to George when the tide of the war
turns and the Germans begin to retreat. The enemy continues its
merciless artillery bombardment of the advancing armies, and
suicide squads of machine gunners try desperately to hold the
British at bay as their comrades evacuate one village after another.

It is the first of November. As George pursues the fleeing Germans, he can hardly guess that an armistice will be declared in less
than two weeks. Since his company is in the vanguard of the British
army, he is faced with the task of leading the way, day and night,
across an unfamiliar terrain, and of taking the brunt of the bombardment and machine-gun fire from the German rear guard. The
predawn hours of the fourth of November find him assembled with
his battalion in a newly captured French village near the Belgian
border where he is awaiting orders for another furious offensive

against the enemy. He is "at the very end of his endurance"; he has "used up the last fraction of his energy and strength"; he has "only one thought—peace" (*DH*, 371). Time is against him as he waits for the battle to begin: "CRASH! Like an orchestra at the signal of a baton the thousands of guns north and south opened up. The night sprang to flickering daylight with the gun-flashes, the earth trembled with shock, the air roared and screamed with shells. Lights rushed up from the German line, and their artillery in turn flamed into action" (*DH*, 371–72).

This attack is the finale of the long symphony. As George once more leads the way across the battlefield amid the din and the smoke, his men fall about him on either side. As he takes cover from the machine-gun fire, he hears one of his wounded runners moaning in agony nearby; and "Something seemed to break in Winterbourne's head. He felt he was going mad, and sprang to his feet. The line of bullets smashed across his chest like a savage steel whip. The universe exploded darkly into oblivion" (*DH*, 372). The symphony is over, the sequel is already known, and no further comment is needed concerning the story.

But it is probable that George would have suffered even more, that his end would have come even earlier, had he been in the German army. Paul Baumer's experiences in Erich Remarque's *All Quiet on the Western Front* suggest that the privations and agonies of the German troops must have been greater than those of the British, especially in view of the fact that the Germans were faced with the double problem of fighting starvation and the enemy at the same time. This difference does not mean that George suffers less than Paul, nor in exactly the same way. Although many of their experiences are strikingly similar, the more complicated nature of George's prewar existence makes it impossible for him to endure the hardships and horrors for the length of time that Paul does. George is unable to share Paul's pleasure in the periods of rest behind the lines or to take delight in an unexpected feast or a chance encounter with a girl, for he has entered the war as a sophisticated young man who is already lonely and disillusioned. Paul, on the other hand, has enlisted as a carefree, mischievous schoolboy in search of adventure, and his loneliness and disillusionment have come as the sole result of his war experiences. The loss of his closest comrades, one by one, has gradually weakened his will to live.[19]

George also believes that the war has shattered his future as a painter; but Paul, who knows no other profession but that of a soldier, has no hope of a new life after the war. Both are distressed by the realization that they have lost the formative years of their lives, that they are caught between two generations of men whose careers have not been impaired by the war, men with whom they cannot hope to compete in the postwar world. This aspect of the predicament of the two young heroes is universal, and this accounts for the international appeal of the two novels.

Death of a Hero is Aldington's best novel. Critics, who have considered it one of the most perceptive novels about World War I, rank it with such books as Hemingway's *A Farewell to Arms* and Remarque's *All Quiet on the Western Front.* An unusual novel, it owes its reputation to the final part where Aldington gives a remarkably realistic account of modern warfare. The earlier parts of the story, dealing with the hero's background and his life before the war, are disproportionately long and comparatively tedious— especially so because the author becomes engrossed in a series of harangues against prewar English society. The section about the literary milieu of London, with satirical sketches of some of the greatest writers of the twentieth century, will continue to appeal to the student of literature rather than to the general reader. Aldington's satire is most effective in the last part of the book, where he relies more upon narrative and dialogue to express his feelings and attitudes, for it is there that the hero becomes a truly symbolic figure of a generation of young men destroyed by a modern war.

II   Roads to Glory

Aldington's *Roads to Glory* (1930), a companion book to *Death of a Hero*, is a collection of short stories that deal with the effects of the war upon various individuals and that provide additional insights into the physical and mental anguish caused by the war. McGreevy accurately describes this work as "a series of postscripts" to the novel;[20] to Snow, it is "full of the truth, courage and despair which no one can miss" in the other book.[21] Although the author makes no such division himself, the stories may be classified into two groups, the war and its aftermath. The first group is concerned with the experiences of soldiers; and, for these men, "roads to glory" has only an ironic meaning, since nothing could be less glorious than the fates of the characters in the stories. The description of human anguish and despair in one story, "At All Costs," is more poignant than any that can be found in the novel, since the victims are men who have no wish, conscious or unconscious, to die.

The command from corps headquarters that they are to hold their undermanned and untenable positions "at all costs" is a death sentence from which there is no hope of escape, for they have to signal their artillery to shorten its barrage as soon as the enemy enters their trench. They accept their fate with horrified equanimity. There are incipient symptoms of panic among the junior officers, who quite innocently attempt to get drunk until their captain intervenes. But this is the only outward sign of weakness, although Captain Hanley himself is in a daze as he carries out his orders. His agony is especially moving as he lies awake in the dark, in a cold sweat, thinking about his wife. When the attack begins, his impressions are conveyed to the reader not as emotions but as a series of stupendous images as the fury of the battle engulfs him.

In "Sacrifice Post," Lieutenant Davison is faced with the same fate as Captain Hanley, but he is temporarily relieved of duty and sent to school for training as a signal officer. The sudden change has a profound effect upon him—one day he is frantically dodging deadly missiles amid the stench and clamor of the trenches, and the next he is resting calmly in a quiet meadow far behind the lines. He is overcome by a feeling of peace and brotherly love for all men; and, as the tranquil days pass, he records his thoughts in his notebook. Unlike Lieutenant Evans in *Death of a Hero,* and thousands of other young British officers, he has a revelation which permits him to see through the pernicious "cant" of his elders: "The trouble was that it was almost impossible for an ordinary uneducated public school man to think coherently, let alone express his feelings. . . . If only he knew more, if only he could make others feel that vision, make them understand how they were duped into hatred under the guise of loyalty and duty!"[22] He is unlucky, nevertheless, in the particular moment that fate has chosen for his enlightenment. The notebook is discovered, and he is returned with tragic results to the advance post on the front line.

Even more pathetic is the case of Harry Werner in "Deserter," a friendless orphan who becomes a victim of the same tyranny which destroys Lieutenant Davison—of a system which has no tolerance for the philosophies of individual men. In "A Bundle of Letters," the author employs the epistolary method to tell the story of a young officer who attempts to circumvent the system by subtle and devious means. Like George Winterbourne, Lieutenant Walter Bracegirdle finds life in the trenches particularly agonizing and detrimental to a man of sensitivity and talent; but, unlike Winterbourne, he does not accept his duty with hopeless resignation. Because of his lack of scruples, he does not arouse the compassion of the reader whose sympathy is shifted to the well-meaning colonel who almost gets into trouble by agreeing to help Bracegirdle. One cannot avoid being touched by the loyalty and understanding which the senior officers give one another, nor by the "poetic justice" of the young man's fate when he receives an injury that puts an end to his career as a pianist.

"Killed in Action" deals with a more sinister, but not unknown form of military "justice." It is the story of two young men, Jack Hann and Eric Crane, who become bitter rivals in the prewar army of professional soldiers. Hann's alacrity in murdering his old comrade is horrifying, as is his lack of any sense of remorse afterward; but it is difficult to censure him for an act which is equivalent to self-defense. As the author implies, the fault lies with the institution which fostered the inhumane rivalry and which also gave one man arbitrary power over another by virtue of his rank.

The second group of stories deals with the returning "heroes." "The Case of Lieutenant Hall" is an account, in the form of entries from a diary, of a man who survives the horrors of the trenches and battlefields only to be destroyed by the intangible horror of his memories. It is a ghost story of sorts, but one without the spine-chilling mystery and suspense which is ordinarily found in such a tale. There is no implication of any supernatural force at work—only a hypersensitive nature and vivid imagination; and the character is dismissed by an unfeeling society simply as a person "of unsound mind."

In "Meditation on a German Grave," which contains many autobiographical details, an ex-officer discovers that he has been ruined by the war. By dint of long hours and hard work, however, he becomes a success within a few years; but he eventually suffers a breakdown from overwork. When his doctor advises him to take a vacation, he decides to spend it on a secluded island in the Mediterranean. In the days that follow, he begins to find peace of mind by living in harmony with the natural beauty of the island and by recollecting the past in tranquillity. His memories of the war, though still painful, are no longer unbearable, for he has his sudden but calm recollection of the feelings of despair which overcame him in a large German cemetery in France shortly before the Armistice. This recollection has the effect of a catharsis; for, as soon as he is able to see the past in its proper perspective, it is no longer a threat to his present or future happiness.

The last piece in the book, "Farewell to Memories," is a sort of fictionalized panorama of the author's experiences during his training camp days, his life at the front, his demobilization, and his return to England; and his emotional responses to the experiences are presented in italicized passages. In view of the fact that more than ten years passed before Aldington recovered sufficiently from the agony of his war experiences to give them complete treatment in writing, and in light of his comment that by writing them down "I purged my bosom of perilous stuff which had been poisoning me for a decade,"[23] there can be no doubt about the cathartic purpose of the two books, *Death of a Hero* and *Roads to Glory;* for, as he says, "I worked . . . the passion and indignation which inspired them . . . out of my system."[24] He was able to return to France again and again, both in real life and in his books; but never again did he dwell upon the war which had been fought there.

The novel and collection of short stories represent Aldington's greatest achievement in prose fiction, and they reveal a comprehensive view of society which has earned them a permanent place among the best of their kind in literature.

CHAPTER 6

The Satirist

*D*EATH *of a Hero* (1929) established Aldington's reputation as a novelist. With the exception of 1935 and 1936, he published a novel or a volume of short stories each year for the next decade, the majority of which have been translated into several languages. Although much of their immediate success may be attributed to the popularity of the first novel, some of them may survive on their own merits. When the controversy dies concerning the man who debunked the legend of Lawrence of Arabia, British and American critics may take a closer and more objective look at some of Aldington's other works.

I The Colonel's Daughter

Aldington's second novel, *The Colonel's Daughter* (1931), is the result of the seven or eight years which he spent in a cottage in rural Berkshire where he retired from London in order to recover from the war.[1] While he admits to "some fancy and caricature" in the book, he insists that it is largely a faithful portrayal of the local inhabitants.[2] He also abandons his experiments in form and structure, since this novel, as well as the others which follow, is conventional in its design and arrangement. *The Colonel's Daughter,* moreover, is less harsh and bitter than the first novel. Although bitterness is quite apparent, it is tempered by the compassion and understanding which the author shows for characters that he would have treated with unconcealed contempt in *Death of a Hero* and also by the fact that he never loses his sense of humor. The Smithers are a middle-class family who have not emancipated themselves from Victorian values and prejudices, chiefly because of their isolation from the centers of postwar civilization; but, since the "old regime of Cant,"[3] which they represent, is dead, they are no longer capable of harming anyone except themselves, although their tragedy must have been a common phenomenon in postwar England. It is probably for this reason that the author limits himself, for the most part, to less direct social satire; for it is expressed in the ridiculous and ineffectual behavior of the characters. Furthermore, while no one can miss the satirical intent of the book, one cannot easily identify the author's own predilections and preferences without reference to his other work; for he carefully avoids any conspicuous intrusion of the author into the story.

Georgina Smithers, the central character of this novel, is the only child of a retired lieutenant colonel and his wife. Fred Smithers, her father, and the embodiment of the soldier-sportsman ideal, yearns for nothing better, now that he can no longer slaughter other men, than to slaughter animals, birds, and fish at will and in abundance. Because of Georgina's family and her own qualities, Georgie, as the daughter is called, has several handicaps in her pursuit of happiness. The most formidable of these is her strict Victorian upbringing which forbids any intimacy with a man unless she is married to him. Her father's affairs with women are irrelevant because she knows nothing of them and because he hypocritically maintains an outmoded decorum in his own home. Georgie is also handicapped by her plain face, although she has a good figure; but she can employ neither to her best advantage since she is not allowed to use cosmetics nor to wear fashionable clothes. These shortcomings, however, would not be insuperable barriers to her happiness if it were not for the comparative poverty of her family. She has a comfortable life at home, but cannot afford to have parties and an automobile, the necessities to a young woman of her station in society if she is to meet and woo eligible young men. To make matters worse, she cannot even expect to be invited to many parties, for she lacks the qualities which would make her popular among others of her own age and class—wit, talent, education, intelligence.

Fate plays a major role in Aldington's writings. Unless the character is wealthy, only the rare one escapes the lot imposed upon him by society, and he must be endowed with exceptional intelligence, sensitivity, and imagination even to hope for escape. Georgie has none of these characteristics and her personal circumstances are such that she can hardly avoid the fate of becoming an old maid; in addition to her own difficulties, a shortage of eligible young men exists in postwar England. In this novel, which is concerned with the most critical months of Georgie's life, events determine the course of her life; and her submissiveness to these events has the effect of sealing her fate.

As the public-school girl counterpart of the public-school boy, Georgie is a member of the Girl Guides, in which she takes much interest in order to escape boredom. Since she is a healthy young woman, she is anxious to find a husband before she passes the prime of her youth. She is "the kind of person who makes a 'good' wife and mother, because she would never have asked for anything but what she was bound to be given—i.e. whatever the prejudices of her class demanded" (*CD*, 21). Moreover, Georgie is not handicapped by impractical considerations in her choice of a husband, for any decent man of her own class, with modest means, will suffice. If she is nothing else, she is so kind and gentle that she does not allow her envy and prejudices to prevent her from doing all she can for her pregnant maid-servant, Lizzie, even in the face of opposition from influential persons in the village.

In Georgie's efforts to help the pregnant girl, Lizzie, she enlists the aid of Purfleet, an intellectual dilettante who has no love for his neighbors but feels sorry for Georgie and Lizzie. Reginald Purfleet is not Richard Aldington, but he is the only character in the novel who shares the author's tastes, interests, and cynicism. Like the author, he is an insatiable reader, a lover of the arts, and a freethinker who hates war, sports, hypocrisy, and everything else associated with the middle-class Establishment; and he, in turn, is feared and disliked by his less sophisticated neighbors. Unlike the author, he is a loquacious idler who is not bound by the necessity of earning a living, and he is also dissociated from identification with Aldington by his latent homosexuality and by his impotence with women. The village doctor, Malcolm McCall, who is Purfleet's only close friend, serves as a sounding board for the latter's wit, as well as for his views concerning his neighbors and the world at large, which in their turn are frequently expressive of the author's own outlook. Since the doctor is an intelligent but not a learned man, "Purfleet's literary graces" are often "wasted upon that solid Scotch intellect" (*CD*, 210); but the waste with him is far less than with Georgie whose almost total lack of comprehension affords much fun and humor in the novel.

In writing *The Colonel's Daughter*, Aldington had no cause to fear, as he did with his first novel, that the reader would be more interested in the plot than in "what I had to say and the way I said it."[4] If he had terminated the story at the point where Purfleet abandons Georgie to boredom and spinsterhood—a reasonable conclusion in view of her marital ambitions and lack of resources—it would still be a good novel because of the skill of the narrative and the richness of the dialogue. It is well, however, that the author does not stop with these accomplishments; for, as entertaining as the various characters and episodes may be, nothing of great consequence has yet occurred; and, as a result, the reader has only an imperfect sense of the tragedy of Georgie's life. The author softens the pathos with his acute wit and sense of humor, which on some occasions remind one of Dickens and on others of Aldous Huxley, although Aldington has too much learning and imagination to imitate any writer. Huxleyan wit is apparent whenever Purfleet appears on the scene, and his "affair" with Georgie is worthy of comparison with such short stories as "After the Fire-works" and with certain episodes in *Crome Yellow* and *Antic Hay*. Dickensian humor characterizes the passages describing the colonel, his wife, and the cousin who lives with them. For example, when Coz tries to seduce Lizzie, he gets such a beating from her that the reader cannot help laughing at and feeling sorry for the poor fellow at the same time. Also humorous are the ludicrous antics of Mrs. Eastcourt (the village gossip), the encounters with Lizzie's father, and the mock-tragic triangle of Bert Wrigley, his gypsy wife, and Farmer Reeves; and the author's familiarity with the speech of the lower classes enriches the humor.

Early in the climactic episode of the novel, the author justifies his use of an improbable situation by the following observation: "Occasionally Nature does appear to do things handsomely—especially when preparing a dirty trick" (*CD*, 263). Until now, Georgie has never really met the "right man" or sought him. She has sought men not for themselves but for the comforts they can provide, and her artless vamping is made all the more pathetic by her innocence and unrealistic expectations. Geoffrey Hunter-Payne *is* the right man—or at least he should have been for Georgie. The author shows a great deal of narrative skill in the way that he leads to the meeting between Georgie and Geoffrey, so that the reader is almost as surprised as the heroine, and he does not tax the reader's credulousness by describing Geoffrey as handsome, although he is robust and moderately good-looking. Most important, Geoffrey is a perfect match. It is not simply "girl meets boy," but adult Girl Guide meets

"adult Boy Scout, a Public School fag in shining armour," as Aldington calls this type of man in *Death of a Hero*.[5] Georgie's ultimate failure with Geoffrey is especially touching and ironic because
she appears to have so many opportunities for success.

In *The Colonel's Daughter*, Aldington appears to show considerable development as a novelist. As Thomas McGreevy observed,
"Not . . . since Lawrence painted the landscape of industrial England in *Sons and Lovers* has there been so richly evocative a picture of the English scene in a book."[6] He also noted that the author
"has not only come home from the war," but "has also brought the
English novel home from the smart cosmopolitan malice of Somerset Maughamism and the arid puritanical hatred of Aldous Hux-
leyism" by creating memorable characters, such as Lizzie's father,
who are "lovable as well as intelligent" and "whose memory one
cherishes as one remembers some sympathetic figure in a picture."[7]
Instead of resorting to invective commentary, moreover, as he did
in the first novel, Aldington allows the reader to form his own
opinions of the characters and their faults through his mildly
humorous descriptions of them and their interactions with one
another. Even in the case of Purfleet, who is not an entirely admirable character, it is not always easy to tell when the author is being
serious or merely ironic. Only in his account of Sir Horace Stimms,
the multimillionaire ruler of the village and the keeper of its morals
(enforced by the unpaid and voluntary services of Mrs. Eastcourt), is
Aldington clearly unambivalent in his sentiments; and, lest the
reader should miss the point in the story, the author has added an
epilogue to remind him of it.

In the novel, Aldington shifts the blame for international dis-
putes, the ills of society in general, and the tragedy of poor Georgie
from middle-class society at large to the moneyed interests of the
nation which are represented by Stimms. Stimms' power and authority in the village is recognized by all its inhabitants: he denies
the colonel the pleasure of hunting, forces the parson to resign,
makes Lizzie's predicament unnecessarily complicated, and
contributes to the general misery of most of the people in the village. In a less personal way, he contributes to one of the causes of
Georgie's misfortunes, since he and other wealthy and powerful
men like him are responsible for getting her "possible husbands
killed, or exiled to look after [their] commercial interests" and there-

fore compels her "to preserve . . . an imaginary virtue she doesn't want" (*CD*, 56–57).

The epilogue is not a continuation of the story, but a phantasmagoria in prose that is reminiscent of *A Fool i' the Forest*. In the epilogue, two fantastical Russian visitors discuss Stimms and his village while picnicking at night on the local soccer field. Their drunken conversation is as fanciful as themselves; and the scene, despite much fustian bombast which is frequently incoherent, is full of sententious observations. Besides explaining Stimms' rise to power as the despot of a village and one of the rulers of an empire, the two aliens also predict the fall of the man and his ill-gotten empire, a fate already prophesied earlier by Purfleet in an impassioned debate with Dr. McCall. Again the author mixes comedy (perhaps "farce" would be a better word) with seriousness in order to maintain the mood of the rest of the novel.

Aldington's anticapitalist bias throughout the book probably explains the popularity of *The Colonel's Daughter* in the Soviet Union, even though the writer does not indicate any definite preference for the ascendant Labor Party of his country—indeed, it is seldom mentioned. He does not appear to be concerned with the establishment of any particular party or form of government, as is implied by Purfleet's "horror . . . of practical politics" (*CD*, 178); but he is concerned about the existence of any regime which permits its wealth and power to fall into the hands of a few men, such as Stimms, who have no genuine regard for the welfare of others.

The Colonel's Daughter is a more skillfully constructed novel than *Death of a Hero*, for the author deals with a slice of life at a moment of crisis and never allows the action to bog down in unnecessary moralizing. If it is not as great a piece of work as *Death of a Hero*, it is because the heroine is more a pathetic figure than a tragic one; for hers is the tragicomic story of an unintelligent and unimaginative young woman who is unable to escape the prejudices of her class in order to avoid the fate of remaining unmarried and unhappy for the rest of her life.

II Soft Answers

During the interim between the appearance of his second and third novels, Aldington published a collection of short stories, *Soft Answers* (1932), which was reprinted in 1967 by the Southern Illinois University Press in its Crosscurrents/Modern Fiction series. In the preface to the 1967 edition, Harry T. Moore observes that all the stories, except "Last Straws," are satires; but they "are not fully satirical if only because none of them makes a big, raging, moral attack on social evils." The stories, instead, tend "to be the kind of personal satires that are perhaps more accurately called carica- tures."[8] To Moore, the author employs "a kind of caricature of the type D. H. Lawrence almost seems to have invented: the lampoon in miniature"; he also explains the nature of this interesting literary phenomenon:

In London in 1950 I discussed this genre with Sir Compton Mackenzie, who had several times been the victim of D. H. Lawrence's pen. . . . He said that Lawrence's fiction of this kind often gave a distorted view of his victims because "he had a trick of describing a person's setting or background vividly, and then putting into the setting an ectoplasm entirely of his own creation." Sir Compton added that those who know these victims will never see the stories as falsifications; but that they would have an artistic validity for other readers who did not know the principals. And this might apply to Aldington's half-satires.

To say as much takes nothing away from their intrinsic worth as stories. . . . At one level the stories belong to the literary history of an epoch; at another level they can be read for their own sake.[9]

Moore also indicates that these stories "contain dynamite," for they include lampoons on some of the most important literary figures of the era, among them T. S. Eliot and Ezra Pound; but he advises the reader to "make his own discoveries" despite his helpful hints.[10] The purpose of this present discussion is not to identify all the characters in the satires (even if it were possible to do so), for doing so would divert attention from what Moore considers the "intrinsic worth" of the stories themselves. Moreover, only the two most renowned of the author's acquaintances, Pound and Eliot, are dis- cussed in relationship to the pieces which focus upon them.

Oswald Carstairs in " 'Yes, Aunt' " is a less admirable person than Purfleet in *The Colonel's Daughter*, whom he resembles in some respects. Both are confirmed bachelors with vague homosexual ten- dencies; and while they are devoted to an appreciation of the arts are wholly unproductive themselves. Oswald, however, is a harm- less, rather ugly little man, with less intelligence and strength of character, and with none of the other's gift for eloquent discourse.

Like George's parents in *Death of a Hero,* Oswald and Julia Carstairs in " 'Yes, Aunt' " are "grotesques" who evoke amusement rather than sympathy, for they are victims of their own vices and get only what they deserve. Constance Lechdale's grotesqueness in "Now She Lies There" is all the more apparent since she has a beautiful face which contrasts sharply with her moral depravity, but the outcome of her willful behavior is so appalling that the story is not even tragicomical.

"Now She Lies There," a serious story, contains far more thoughtful commentary than humor. The setting in which the narrator tells his tale is a gloomy one, since a fierce winter storm has been raging all night outside the little cottage where he lives alone; and this introduction creates an entirely different mood than that of the previous story. It forbodes real disaster with as much certainty as the opening pages of a gothic novel, and any humor found would be gratuitous comic relief.

Constance drinks and dances her way across Europe with an abandon which reminds one of Lady Brett Ashley in *The Sun Also Rises.* The narrator's comment that she "is the wreck of a noble woman" (*SA*, 45) suggests a tragedy in the Aristotelian sense of the word, but it is difficult to pity a person who has wantonly tormented and destroyed others merely to amuse herself, no matter how harsh her fate may be. Only in a larger sense is she truly a tragic figure; for, like the hero and heroine of the author's first two novels, she is a representative of the generation destroyed by the war. As the narrator explains,

I remembered how Constance had often seemed to me a symbolical figure, an embodiment of the post-War plutocracy and its jazz Dance of Death. Well, the plaster visage had fallen off the Death's Head in her case. Only it wasn't a complete death, any more than the dance had been a real dance. It was the kind of death where you remain sufficiently alive to know you are dead—the most horrible kind. It struck me that a similar fate had already descended on Constance's epoch and companions, the bored revellers who had caroused so drearily over the graves. No sudden catastrophe had overwhelmed them, no grand conflict in which they could at least die nobly. They had simply got drunk once too often and lost their money—the blood money of the dead legions. They had had their little day and danced their dance, and the world had grown weary of them. It hadn't even bothered to scratch them off, but left them to drop away one by one, like aged parasites. My feeling was one of serenity and hope, as if a sickness were ending, and health was in sight. (*SA*, 86–87)

This comment is as good as one can probably find about the reckless madness of the "lost generation" of the "roaring twenties." "Now She Lies There" is an excellent piece of work. This judgment does not apply, however, to *Life of a Lady* (1936), a play based on the story and written by Aldington and Derek Patmore. The dramatized story is absurd and melodramatic, but its original is a credit to the author.

A different result of war is portrayed in "A Gentleman of England," the story of Harold Formby-Pett, an unscrupulous businessman who rises from moderate middle-class comfort to opulence on the tide of the industrial boom created by the war. His wife, Esther, becomes the heroine of the story and acts as the author's spokesman in denouncing her husband and the type of man he symbolizes. By means of her impassioned outbursts, the author manages to levy an assault on the unscrupulous financiers of the world in a way that he was unable to accomplish with his references to Sir Horace Stimms in *The Colonel's Daughter* or his direct commentary in the *Death of a Hero*. Esther's denunciation is unobtrusive because the dialogue in which it appears is an integral part of the story about her husband. Any direct commentary in the story is also addressed strictly to Harold, and such a comment is always softened by a pervasive ironic humor which precludes an overly serious attitude toward him or the other characters.

Aldington's irreverent attitude toward Christianity has been mentioned in the chapters dealing with his poetry and first novel. It is also apparent in "A Gentleman of England," where some of the humor depends on the reader's ability to laugh at sacred matters. The author does not attack Christian beliefs per se, but provides an extended allegory on Harold's "religion of Money," which he feels has replaced Christianity in the lives of some people. Moreover, lest Aldington be accused of anti-Semitism in his treatment of Rosengrab, Harold's partner, the following comments by Esther are worth consideration: "Why, without Rosengrab you were as helpless and gullible as a child, or a woman. . . . You despised him because he was a Jew, and you were a gentleman with a school tie and an accent. But he had the Jew's suppleness and toughness and the Jew's intelligence. You hadn't. You were as weak as your Blood and as flabby as your Breeding' " (*SA*, 159–60). If Rosengrab cannot be admired because of his dishonesty, he is at least less despicable than Harold in the story; he possesses some qualities that might have

produced a great man in other circumstances. Aldington expresses
warm admiration for Jews elsewhere in his writings, as in "Meditation on a German Grave" in which the partner in the business is a
young man (apparently based on a friendship in the author's own
life)[11] with every bit of Rosengrab's shrewdness and intelligence but
with none of his greediness or dishonesty.

In the other two satires, Aldington turns to pure fun and levity.
"Nobody's Baby," subtitled "a mystery story," is a frivolous lampoon
on Ezra Pound, who is the center of attraction, the character with
the incredible name of Charlemagne Cox who is a musician—a circumstance which would lead one to believe that the author desired
to cast Pound (who is portrayed as a painter in *Death of a Hero*) in
every artistic role except the literary one for which he is most famous. At any rate, it is not too hard to recognize Pound as a musician, for, as Moore points out, he "was usually involved in avant-
garde music as well as poetry."[12] Murray Schafer, a musicologist
who has written a brilliant essay explaining Pound's interest in
music and its influence on his poetry, mentions Pound's own musical compositions, among them "an opera, *Le Testament*, which, if
better known, would have been one of the most controversial pieces
of music of its epoch."[13] As is Aldington's custom, he distorts
Pound's actual interests and accomplishments in such a way that no
one should misconstrue the story as having any serious intent, as
containing any sober criticism of the man or his work.

Cox's program for his recital that occurs at the beginning of the
story includes such bizarre pieces as "Renderings from a second-
century papyrus," "Bantu tom-tom Symphony," and "Harold
Harada, an OPERA" (further identified as "Fragments of his great
musical work in progress"), all "arranged for the piano by CHAR-
LEMAGNE COX" (*SA*, 90). Pound's own opera, fragments of which
were performed in Paris in 1924 and 1926, is an adaptation to music,
composed by him, of the ballades of François Villon because of his
interest in medieval French poetry and music.[14] The Bantu tom-
tom symphony and Cox's impromptu performance later on an "Afri-
can drum" (*SA*, 97) are probably based on a concert at which Pound
actually played a "big bass drum."[15] Cox's heterogeneous collection
of instruments also reflects Pound's use of unusual musical devices
in the production of his opera.[16]

In this portrayal of Cox, Aldington exaggerates Pound's mannerisms even more than he does in *Death of a Hero*, especially his

conceit, aggressiveness, cough, nervous movements, American dialect, enigmatic utterances, and bohemian attire. The author's attempts to imitate American speech, here and elsewhere, are much less skillful and effective than his reproduction of English dialect in his writings, but Cox's query, "Is he dong le mouvemong?" (SA, 93) is a dead giveaway of the character's identity.[17] It is also possible—though this hypothesis is unprovable—that Pound would have been a failure, as Cox is, had he chosen music instead of poetry as his favorite medium of artistic expression.

The story, however, is not primarily concerned with either Pound's or Cox's artistic interests and achievements: it is a "mystery story" concerning the identity of a baby's parents. Cox's wife and mother-in-law seem to bear some resemblance to the women in Pound's life, and both men, who were married just before the war, remained childless for many years afterward.[18] Since the announcement of the birth of a daughter to Cox and his wife amazes some of his acquaintances, who have long been convinced that he is impotent, two of them make a small wager as to whether the baby exists; and the sport of "Cox-hunting" begins. The search for the child and its parents is described in an amusing manner, and the mystery is solved at the end of the story.

Moore states that he has "as yet found no proof that the story about Pound . . . really angered him," and he adds that the great poet "remained Aldington's friend, writing him frequently toward the end of Aldington's life, at a time when so many of his fellow writers were shunning him."[19] T. S. Eliot, on the other hand, was greatly offended by Aldington's treatment of him in "Stepping Heavenward," as this quotation indicates:

Richard was very sensitive, not to say touchy, in some ways and I am afraid that with good intentions, but clumsy lack of imagination, I hurt his feelings once or twice very deeply indeed. After that, I saw nothing of him and he wrote a cruel and unkind lampoon of me and of my wife who died some years later, and of friends of mine such as Lady Ottoline Morrell and Virginia Woolf. . . . But that quarrel had since subsided and I exchanged letters with him a few years before his death. . . . I . . . have nothing left but feelings of friendliness and regard. . . . We were on the same side for a long time and I was the first to give offense, although unintentionally, which made a breach between us.[20]

In contrast to the plausible nature of the other satires, "Stepping Heavenward" is an utterly fabulous account of an incredible character; but any reader who is at all acquainted with Eliot's life can hardly fail to recognize him as the subject of the story because the parallels, superficial though many of them may be, between the real man and the fictitious one are so numerous. In the story, Aldington adopts the pose of an impartial biographer in tracing the first forty years or so of the life of one Jeremy Pratt Cibber (formerly Sybba), O. S. B., from his birth to his conversion to Roman Catholicism, with brief mention of his subsequent life, death, and beatification by the pope. The story is diffused with the lightness of tone which is characteristic of the Horatian brand of satire, and its primary purpose is to entertain the reader.

Cibber's birthplace, Colonsville, is readily recognized as Eliot's own St. Louis, while his descent from a New England "aristocracy" (*SA*, 168–69) is a reference to Eliot's distinguished family connections and ancestry. Cibber's enrollment in an unnamed private academy in Colonsville and later in "the great nation-famous university of Kail" (*SA*, 179–80) also correspond, respectively, to Eliot's attendance of Smith Academy (St. Louis) and Harvard. Except in broad outline, however, the account of Cibber's childhood appears to have little in common with that of Eliot; but it is a humorous, if imaginary, effort by the author to explain the origin of some of the traits of Eliot. His "monosyllabic reserve" (*SA*, 178) and his repression of "not only the outward expression of emotion but emotion itself, until nothing remains but the pure intellect and the pure spirit of contemplation" (*SA*, 180), are gross exaggerations of the "sang-froid" demeanor which the author observed in his relations with Eliot.[21] These traits are emphasized in the scene in which Cibber's father is mourning the death of his wife and has difficulty eliciting any response but a cool Eliotic "Yes?" or "Indeed?" from his son, who also corrects any error in his parent's literary allusions (*SA*, 180–82). As in *Death of a Hero*, Aldington caricatures Eliot's speech and mannerisms.

In fact, Aldington exaggerates and fabricates Eliot's life wherever doing so pleases him. Early in his life, Cibber decides to become "The Poet Laureate" or "The Historiographer Royal" of England (*SA*, 177). Possibly to avoid too close a parallel with Eliot's life, Aldington chooses to make his character an historian, though he has him change his name from Sybba to Cibber in honor of the laureate who was the butt of some of Alexander Pope's satire. Cibber spends a year in postgraduate work at the Sorbonne, as Eliot had done; later, in London, he renews his acquaintance with Lucas Cholmp, who cannot be mistaken for anyone but Ezra Pound. Aldington's implication of resentment appears in a passage which refers to Eliot's relationship with the imagists since Aldington and Pound were leading figures in this group: "Cholmp did work hard to establish his protégé in England . . . by introducing him to the New School of historians. In this way, Cibber was early made acquainted with important pioneer work. . . . These young men were arranging for the publication of a joint work. . . . Cibber did not join the enterprise. . . . In private, however, he made a number of notes in which the faults of each of his new friends were brought out with masterly incisiveness" (SA, 194–95). This statement is aimed rather directly at Eliot, who not only did not ally himself with the imagists, but was critical of their work and wrote articles which often opposed their theories and aggravated the members of the group.[22] At the same time, as Aldington has pointed out elsewhere, Eliot's own accomplishments have owed much to groundwork done by the imagists.[23]

When Cibber meets Cholmp and a companion upon his return from Switzerland, he is "wearing a new ceremonial bowler . . . and a short but goat-like beard, which he had suffered in Geneva" (SA, 194). This reference is to the occasion when Aldington introduced Eliot to Bruce Richmond, the editor of The Times Literary Supplement: "and in came Tom—wearing, if you please, a derby hat and an Uncle Sam beard he had cultivated in Switzerland."[24] Cibber also teaches for a time, as did Eliot; but the account of his marriage appears to be a fabrication for the most part, aside from the fact that Cibber's, like Eliot's, is a very unhappy one. Cibber's employment in a haberdashery, "where his courteous manners and distinguished appearance found full scope" (SA, 198), is a humorous allusion to Eliot's position in Lloyd's Bank. Cibber's "epoch-making Notes on the Provincial Itinerary of the Emperor Antoninus," with its "contemplation of the grave and the scurry of rats over the withered hopes of Mankind" (SA, 201–2), is a reference to The Waste Land and its voluminous notes. Cibber's "Notes" establish his reputation as an historian, much in the same way that The Waste Land brought Eliot fame as a poet; and Cibber too becomes a highly controversial figure: "Within a year Cibber was the acknowledged if unofficial Social-intellectual dictator of England" (SA, 204). The remark, however, that Cibber "ought to read a little philosophy" (SA, 205) is an intentional absurdity, for Eliot had done doctoral work in philosophy and had written an acceptable dissertation in that field.

Cibber's advocacy of royalism and his search for religion also have their counterparts in Eliot's life. He too becomes a naturalized British subject, and his conversion to Roman Catholicism parallels Eliot's adoption of the Anglo-Catholic faith; but the occasion of Cibber's sudden conversion—when his wife elopes with another man—is fictitious relative to Eliot, as is his retirement to a monastery and the additional conversion, through his example, of millions of people "in sobbing masses" (*SA*, 208), including the duchess and Mrs. Myrrhwell, who are probably identifiable as two of Eliot's friends, Lady Ottoline Morrell and Virginia Woolf.

Throughout the story, Aldington's frivolous treatment of Christianity is even more direct and pervasive than in "A Gentleman of England." But his mild satire mocks at sacred things without attacking them, and his gibes are generally too absurd to be taken seriously. While some readers may find these passages offensive, they are only one more indication of the levity of the entire account, which begins and ends as an extravaganza of the imagination.

Although Moore asks "why did Aldington caricature his old friend, T. S. Eliot?"[25] Aldington was both amused and irritated by some of the eccentricities of his American colleagues, Pound and Eliot, and he could not help feeling that they were upstarts by the manner in which they tried to dominate the English literary scene. He felt that Eliot's masquerade as an Englishman was as ludicrous as Ford Madox Ford's pretensions to being a German aristocrat.[26] Artificiality or insincerity always aroused his contempt, and he was no doubt appalled by Eliot's enthusiastic espousal of a nation, a church, and a set of prejudices which he himself despised. On more than one occasion when the two men were together, Eliot's behavior embarrassed Aldington and offended his British sensibilities. Though Aldington liked and admired both Eliot and Pound, as his writings testify, his respect and admiration for Eliot appears to have diminished even less with the passage of time than his regard for Pound. In his autobiography, he acknowledges the achievement of Eliot, who "by merit, tact, prudence, and pertinacity . . . succeeded in doing what no other American has ever done—imposing his personality, taste, and even many of his opinions on literary England."[27] Additional praise of Eliot appears in the same book, but it is not uncritical praise, and the author includes two or three amusing anecdotes about him. Aldington was incapable of idolatry when writing about his friends, but it is possible that he may have *tried* to do more to assist Eliot in his career than the latter did for him.[28] At any rate, although Aldington probably wrote the lampoon of Eliot in good-natured fun, his taking this liberty with his friend turned out to be unappreciated.

The final story in the book, "Last Straws," is not a satire. As in the case of "Stepping Heavenward," it was published separately before its inclusion in the collection. Its first date of publication was 1930, the same year that *Roads to Glory* appeared, and, in some respects, it belongs to that group of stories, since it is a tragic story about Rawdon, an ex-soldier who has been unable to forget the war and adapt himself to the conditions of peace. Aldington expresses very sensitively the human loneliness and despair which a man must often struggle against alone; for, though Rawdon's friends mean well, they are unable to sympathize fully enough to help him. Their English public-school training, as well as his own, is too formidable a barrier between the best of friends; it causes them to feel inadequate and embarrassed in the presence of another who has lost self-control. This same situation is brought out clearly in *Death of a Hero*, where George Winterbourne and Lieutenant Evans strive to the last to prove their courage and manhood to themselves and others, even when their sufferings are almost unbearable. Apart from the deaths of individual men, Aldington gives us a hint of what may be an even greater tragedy—the inability of men to be true friends to one another for fear of shame or ridicule.

III   All Men Are Enemies

In *All Men Are Enemies* (1933), Aldington seeks a solution to the tragic insensitivity which human beings display in their relationships with one another. His prefatory note explains his aim in the book, for he not only indicates that "every novel which ventures beyond plain storytelling" expresses "a conception of life" (*AM*, v) but also presents his distinction between a modern novel and a modern romance:

I call this book "A Romance" because for me Antony Clarendon is an example of the modern romantic idealistic temperament. A realist in his position would have settled down to a comfortable business career and a get-along-somehow marriage with Margaret. But Antony, like many of us, is an ordinary fallible human being struggling towards what he believes to be a finer and fuller life. In this struggle he holds to two instinctive beliefs which I willingly allow to be romantic: First, that the complete human being is formed by a man and a woman; second, that living implies much more than acquiescence in a set of formal beliefs, more than getting and spending money. Just as he abandons the secular religions of Nationalism, Socialism, and Communism, so he abandons a false marriage and a false career. (*AM*, v–vi)

Aldington also explains that a man's "finer fuller life" is "life with the woman he really loves," and "the energy and beauty of existence which he wants to contribute to their joint possession." He adds that this "is the life of the here and now, the life of the senses, the life of the deep instinctive forces" (*AM*, vi).

This statement expresses Aldington's most cherished conception of life—his "credo," as C. P. Snow calls it.[29] Aldington did not begin his career with a complete knowledge of the "finer fuller life" which he wanted to live himself and express in literature; but his earlier life, poetry, and prose show the steady progress of his thoughts and feelings in the direction of his goal. There are elements of his ultimate ideal in many of his short poems, in *Death of a Hero*, and in two or three of his short stories (especially in "Meditation of a German Grave"). He still searches for it in his first three long poems—*A Fool i' the Forest, A Dream in the Luxembourg,* and *The Eaten Heart*—but, in Snow's opinion, *All Men Are Enemies* "is the fullest expression" of Aldington's "credo."[30] In his last two long poems, however, Aldington does the same thing in verse: *Life Quest* (1935) is an account of his discovery of the ideal, and *The Crystal World* (1937) is more or less the poetic equivalent of his prose romance. In addition, Aldington's autobiography is, as previously noted, the story of his pursuit of the ideal in real life.

Snow notes a "Lawrentian echo" in the author's allusion in *All Men Are Enemies* to "the life of the deep instinctive forces," but he adds that "Aldington's vitalism is different in quality from Lawrence's, and would have been substantially the same if Lawrence had never lived."[31] This view is probably true, for Aldington's total conception of life is his own. Moreover, this novel is certainly not a Lawrentian one, nor could it be mistaken as one, for the feelings which are expressed are not the same as Lawrence's. Indeed, Aldington's early "Greek dream" is more apparent in *All Men Are Enemies* than in *Death of a Hero*. In the latter book, the dream is recalled in a long paragraph where the author fills the scene of George's childhood with the gods and demigods of Greek mythology; and it is also found in the narrator's apostrophes to the gods of

Greece, especially to Aphrodite, during George's courtship of Elizabeth. As McGreevy asserts, "One must not, I think, see a continuation of Lawrence's utopian belief in a sexual earthly paradise in the apostrophes to Aphrodite in *Death of a Hero*," since "they show a wider knowledge and understanding of human experience in the matter than Lawrence."[32]

Whether Aldington shows "wider knowledge and understanding" is debatable, his "belief in a sexual earthly paradise" is more a personal matter than a social one, and he has no "utopian" illusions of a society where all can share his conception of life. Aldington believes that each individual must seek his own paradise within the confines of the existing social organization and that this person must find one member of the opposite sex with whom he can share his deepest desires and feelings. Though the pair will be much happier if they can escape from social pressures and dwell in beautiful surroundings, they cannot seek the "finer fuller life" by forming a colony of "life-seekers"; for, though their paradise is as exclusive as the Garden of Eden, such a paradise is more a matter of a shared state of mind than of a physical environment. Aldington's gods, moreover, are the Hellenic divinities of nature, not the mysterious dark gods in whom Lawrence professes to believe. For Aldington, they are symbols of the natural forces and beauty of the world— symbols of "the real holy ones/ Sun Sea and Earth."[33]

Part 1 of *All Men are Enemies*, which deals with Antony Clarendon's childhood and young adulthood, focuses upon his life from 1900 to 1914. As the story opens on Mount Olympus, a council of the gods has convened to discuss Antony's approaching birth. The Homeric echo of the narrative and dialogue is appropriate here, for it is not Antony's destiny to live as other men do; for, as Zeus prophesies, he is "to struggle ever for a life like unto our own and to suffer defeat from men's evil" (*AM*, 3–4). This council of the gods performs much the same function as the Prologue in *Death of a Hero*, since the author is again revealing the plot at the beginning of the story, according to the custom of the Greek writers of tragedies.[34] But the exposition of Antony's fate is handled more artistically: it is much briefer, it does not interfere with the structure of the plot, and it leaves ample room for suspense and surprise as the story unfolds.

The gods vanish, and the scene shifts suddenly to Vine House in rural England where Antony is born. Unlike George in *Death of a*

Hero, Antony grows up in perfect harmony with his surroundings, as the ideal man should. The story of Antony's prewar life is a modern English idyll, often pastoral in scene and mood, that reflects the peace and tranquillity of a bygone England:

On calm days, especially when the songbirds had ceased, the terrace seemed to be cupped in an immense stillness between motionless trees. If you sat perfectly quiet for long enough there seemed to be no time any more, but a sense of unlapsing existence; no space, but only an airy pattern of colours. It seemed as if you had only to lift a finger to touch the high treetops, to stretch out an arm and you could caress the smooth grass of the distant hill. But you must not move; movement broke the enchantment of strange presences. A butterfly would come across the lawn, either the swift flutter, poise, drop, flutter of the tawny speckled *Vanessidae* or the rambling flicker of the whites. Then would come the sharp, startling squawk of a blue jay from the coppice, or the flat jingle of sheep bells, or the clop-clip-clop, clop-clip-clop of a horse trotting along the hard white road. And then once more you slipped back into the timeless, spaceless world with its scent of cut drying grass and distant fruits. (*AM*, 8–9)

Anyone who has experienced these sensations will feel the beauty and nostalgia of the passage, and there are many scenes such as this one in the book. Antony is happiest at these moments, and he never loses his capacity for intense enjoyment of the natural beauty of the world.

The simple, earthy ways of English country folk are expressed by Antony's nurse, Annie, and her tales of life "down home"; and his visit with her family is as touching and as amusing as David Copperfield's first visit to Peggotty's home. Since no details about Antony's life at school are presented, this omission indicates its lack of importance in the formation of his character. Aldington found his own public-school training a waste of time and irrelevant to his preparation for manhood and a career, and he has George make the same discovery in *Death of a Hero* as does Antony in this novel: "Just as there are two intermingled lives in each person, one of the obvious social man, the other of the mysterious unique personality, so there are two educations, one of formal tuition, the other of unconscious influence; and in each case the latter is by far the more important. Not until much later in life did Antony realize the education of his senses and feelings which came from Vine House and the country in which it stood" (*AM*, 9).

Similar observations are contained in Aldington's autobiography and in his first novel, for he believes that the English public school is inimical to the development of a man of sensitivity and artistic temperament. George escapes the public-school influence through relentless willpower, for unhappiness at home makes him more susceptible to this influence. Although Antony does not have this problem, both boys are dependent upon the counterinfluence of a rural environment and the leisure to enjoy it, as well as upon the presence of good books and an intellectual atmosphere in their homes. In spite of Antony's preference for reading books and communing with nature, he is not a sissy or a weakling; he is proficient at such outdoor sports as cricket and horseback riding. Aldington is not opposed to sports, but to "that grotesque cult of sport which turns so much of country England into a Valhalla of barbarians" (AM, 33). He believes that physical exercise is necessary to the development of the complete man, but he also feels that the emphasis on sports in the English public schools has a tendency to stunt a man's intellectual growth and to dull his sensitivities. Antony is a typical Aldingtonian hero because he does not permit his experiences at school to interfere with the "finer fuller life" which he is unconsciously seeking.

Notwithstanding the simplicity of nurse Annie's mind and character, she has a strong influence on Antony. Long after she is gone, his "vision of Annie" guides his sexual fantasies:

He almost believed that if he put aside the smooth glittering lilac leaves he would catch a glimpse of a white fleeting body which would have breasts like Annie's, round, firm, and white, with the red-brown tips flushed brighter with the sun. How lovely it would be to see a girl's body naked in the sun, with the shadows of lilac leaves trembling over her skin as they rustled in the air. And how more than lovely to hold the cool breasts cupped in his hands and feel their life flow into his fingers as his flowed out in answer, and to taste their texture and odour with his sensitive lips. (AM, 37)

This image is equal to any found in Aldington's love poems. Aldington believes that sexual desire should be beautiful, and his descriptions of a woman's body or a physical act of love are almost always filled with great tenderness and beauty, whether in prose or in verse. There is a sublime quality in Antony's adolescent love affair with his older cousin, Evelyn, who shapes his future attitude toward women and his relations with them.

Like George in *Death of a Hero,* Antony does not choose his closest friends from among his classmates at school, preferring the company of older men. One of these is a militant young Marxist, Stephen Crang, who arouses Antony's concern for the problems of society. Another young man, Robin Fletcher, tries to interest him in a more utopian form of socialism; and he suggests that the two of them found an agrarian colony together. Before long, however, Antony begins to sense the futility of establishing a perfect society; and he abandons the ideas of both men for a more attractive one proposed by an adventurous old country squire—"live your life with gusto." On one occasion, Antony becomes angry and denounces the abuses of modern governments: 'The state is evil. The state doesn't mean the common good, it means governments and executive staffs. . . . States encourage breeding because they want slaves and soldiers. The Socialist state would regulate breeding in order to produce an infinite series of healthy obedient imbeciles living in state houses on state food brought by state transport in order to serve the state, and thus be reduced to a state of state stagnation. To hell with the state' " (*AM,* 130–31).

Later, Antony also dismisses communism as the answer to men's problems: 'I think Communism in practice is poisonous bunk. I don't believe in the class war. I hate it, as I hate all war and killing. The alleged dictatorship of the proletariat is such a swindle that only the proletariat would swallow it. In practice it's the dictatorship of a junta of unscrupulous quasi-scientific fanatics, who'll turn human society into a desert of ennui. . . . I'm concerned with my own individual life, and at least I'll say this for Capitalism, it doesn't wholly prevent my having one' " (*AM,* 325–26).

The foregoing quotations are further examples of Aldington's contempt for politics. Though he does not preach anarchy, Aldington believes that the best government is the least government; and he desires above all to remain aloof from political squabbles and to be left alone as much as possible; he wants no unnecessary bureaucratic interference in the management of his affairs. His unqualified dismissal of socialism and communism in *All Men Are Enemies* makes one wonder, nevertheless, at the great popularity of the book in the Soviet Union,[35] where, according to Mikhail Urnov, sales of its translation have much exceeded even those of *Death of a Hero* in recent years.[36] As Urnov points out, the book did have a "varied reception" in his country at first, but it "withstood criticism." He goes on to say, "The rhapsodical account of how feelings are awakened and how they mature, the hero's spiritual searching, the dramatic love story, the writer's sincere, painful confessions, his exposure of social injustice, the robbery of wartime and the predatoriness of the postwar world—all this attracted the Soviet reader, as it still does, and it is given its due by literary experts."[37] Another Soviet scholar, Dilyara Zhantieva, states that the readers of her nation have been "moved" by the novel's "portrayal of real love, by its pure attitude towards woman and respect for her," adding that the author "will always be remembered" in her country "as a great humanist writer and a man of integrity."[38]

Antony's trip to the remote Mediterranean isle of Aeaea (which takes its name from the island of the enchantress Circe in the *Odyssey*) recalls Aldington's own visits to Capri where he wrote much of the novel.[39] Few of the author's poetic images are more exquisite than the scene where Antony's boat approaches the island in the early morning sunlight. Aldington's botanical knowledge also enhances the account of Antony's drive up the steep slopes of the little isle, and his first stroll outside the tiny mountain village is a description of a pastoral paradise. In a romance, however, so much natural beauty is incomplete without the presence of a lovely woman with whom one can enjoy it. Katha, an Austrian girl whom Antony meets on the island, is not only beautiful, but her naturalness and spontaneity are the qualities which Antony has dreamed of finding in a woman. There is also much of the sublimity of the affair with Evelyn in their almost virginal passion.

In the account of these prewar years, no one can fail to notice that Antony, despite his admirable qualities, is a precocious idler, and that he has led a sheltered and unproductive life in the middle-class Victorian milieu which the author so vigorously condemns in *Death of a Hero*. But Aldington has become more concerned with the ways in which individuals use their privileges than with the exposure of the weaknesses of society. *The Colonel's Daughter* and some of the stories in *Soft Answers* indicate this shift of emphasis, as do *All Men Are Enemies* and the later novels. Aldington acknowledges that some people, regardless of their backgrounds and opportunities, make wiser use of their lives than others; and wisdom is the gift which he has had Athena bestow upon Antony at birth. Nevertheless, Antony's idle dreams and dilettante proclivities leave doubt as to his ability to continue to enjoy the delights which he has discovered.

The first part of the romance, ending with Antony's parting from Katha, shows Aldington at his best. The lyrical quality of the narrative, the vivid description of the scenes, and the passion of the lovers all unite to produce an excellent piece of work. Although the author maintains a nostalgic mood, nothing mawkishly sentimental or melodramatic occurs in the way he tells the story. The proportions of narrative and dialogue are well balanced, and no unnecessary details or digressions interfere with the movement of the action. In fact, the author deals almost too briefly with the relationship between Antony and Katha, implying much more than he says or lets them say, leaving the reader with a fleeting, haunting memory as the story continues.

Part 2, which opens in March, 1919, is preceded by scraps of doggerel verse which satirize each of the intervening years. A sudden, remarkable change in tone is at once apparent. Pursued by phantom skeletons in German uniforms, Antony awakes in a cold sweat; and the gothic gloom of his nightmare lingers in the big, dark, windowless room where "dark flakes of snow" are falling silently on the gray skylight *(AM,* 149–50). Antony has just returned to London from the front, and his agony and restlessness during the long, sleepless night offer the greatest possible contrast to the rapture and tranquillity from which he has just emerged in Part 1. The sudden contrast between the bright ecstasy of Aeaea in the spring of 1914 and the dark despair of London in the winter of 1919 is well portrayed in the vivid scenes and by their attendant moods. Aldington creates the impression of perpetual springtime in the first part of the book, despite the change of seasons; but the gloom of winter overshadows the second part. The curse of Artemis has already been partly fulfilled in the wreck of Antony's life, and the curse of Isis is realized as he begins a long, sad pilgrimage in search of Katha and his lost youth.

The detailed account of Antony's long night in Part 2 is excellent because it sets the tone for the events which follow; for even Aeaea is bleak and cheerless when Antony revisits the island in late autumn. While scenic description is less elaborate than in Part 1, the author's choice of details is always appropriate to the mood. Furthermore, Antony's repeated failures to reestablish his prewar friend-

ships build gradually and effectively to the climax where he finds
that he has lost even Katha, the most important contact with the
happiness of his youth. In other respects, the second part of the
book is not handled as well as the first. The author is often guilty of
disrupting the action by including unessential details or by dwelling
too long on matters which do not require much explanation, such as
Antony's views on life and politics, with the consequence that the
reader finds himself in nearly as great a fever of impatience as
Antony is about the search for Katha.

Part 3 shares the same strengths and weaknesses as Part 2. The
story is taken up again on New Year's Eve of 1926, and Antony has
all but forgotten Katha during his six years of marriage to
Margaret—indeed, there is never any mention of Katha's name in
this part of the book. Part 3 begins well, however. The tenuous
thread connecting the past with the present is skillfully established
at once when Antony abandons other people for a few minutes at a
party:

> Antony did not return directly to the drawing room; . . . the whimsey
> came to him to consult the Homeric lots for a hint of his fate to come. . . .
> He . . . took down his old school Odyssey. . . . He opened the book at
> random and dabbed his finger on a line. . . .
> "And for you, may the Gods grant you to see your wife and to reach your
> home, since for a long time you have endured misfortunes far from your
> friends." (AM, 293–94)

It is soon apparent that Antony is dissatisfied with his present life
and that the languor of the upper middle classes—their inability to
live their lives "with gusto"—finally drives him into open rebellion.

Most of the passages which lead to Antony's decision to make a
break with his present life are well written and essential to the
plot—the New Year's scene, the conversation with Helen
Cartwright, the long walk in March, the company board meeting in
April when he submits his resignation, and the preparations for a
journey abroad. The discussion of his decision with Margaret's
brother Julian also fits in well, even though it is extended beyond a
reasonable limit. A similar talk with an old war comrade and his
"rambling" (the author's own adjective) letter to Julian (AM, 361)
along the same lines, however, could have been omitted, or at least
adumbrated, with no loss to the understanding of Antony's feelings

and motives. These protracted dialogues and monologues are noticeable in Part 2, and they become increasingly apparent in Part 3 and throughout the rest of the book. Instead of contributing to the development of the story, they tend to vitiate the work as a whole and to obscure some of the better passages. This criticism does not mean that Antony (or the author) has nothing more to say, but that he continues to enlarge upon ideas which have been adequately expressed in the first part of the book, repeating his former thoughts in the context of his new insights.

Antony's two-month excursion in France is the most consequential event which takes place in Part 3. As the author points out earlier, Antony has suffered two spiritual deaths: one in the war and the other during his second trip to Aeaea, and on both occasions he has come close to committing suicide. After his first "death" he sets forth in a futile attempt to recapture the life of the past among the shades of the present, only to discover that everyone he has known is now dead to him, and his departure from Aeaea makes him feel "as if he were a dead soul ferried over the waters of death and gazing back at the last glimpse of the warm land of the living" (*AM*, 287). In choosing not to die in body as well as in spirit, he finds that he must forget the past and start life anew, even though doing so means accepting a second-best existence at the expense of the "finer fuller life" of which he has dreamed. Antony's six years with Margaret and her uncle's company give him time for his wounds to heal and to realize that the pursuit of his dream must begin again at the point where he first visited Paris: he must have no tragic memories that could spoil the sense of the adventure before him. It is early April when Antony goes to France, where he begins a long journey on foot across rural France. His pilgrimage southward to meet the spring is symbolic of his desire to return to the springtime of his youth. There is little description of this lengthy journey; but it is clear that, after many years, Antony is once again in harmony with the world about him, although his new life has taken "a mature instead of a youthful shape" (*AM*, 360).

Aldington would have done well to let the episode of Antony's walk from Tours to the Pyrenees serve as the climax of this part of his romance, and he would have done even better to have merged Part 3 and Part 4 and to have excluded at the same time all unnecessary details, dialogue, and commentary. For example, he involves

Antony in the general strike upon the latter's return to England; and his long description of this historical event, while interesting in itself, does not have much relevance to the plot of the story.

In spite of the author's continued prolixity in Part 4, this section gives an account of a fascinating series of events and recaptures much of the drama and beauty found at the beginning of the book. This part of the story opens in February, 1927; and the reader's attention is arrested at once by Antony's discovery of a letter from Evelyn, the older cousin who was his first love and whom he has not seen for eighteen years. As in the case of the reunions mentioned in the discussion of Part 2, the one with Evelyn is also a disappointment, for the natural and uninhibited girl has become a shallow and self-conscious matron. Just when it would appear that Antony has laid the last of the ghosts of his prewar years to rest, after meeting with Evelyn, he learns that Katha has returned to Aeaea. His race against time to reach the island before she leaves is suspenseful, and the description of the scenic beauty of the island compares with that of his first arrival thirteen years earlier. Their reunion is touching without excessive sentimentality, and, if the two lovers do not entirely recover the springtime of their youth, they have a much better chance of realizing their dreams than before. The final curse of Artemis has also been fulfilled when Antony discovers that Katha can no longer bear children, but this is only a minor disappointment since he anticipates the years ahead and is assured that his long and painful odyssey has ended—as foretold by the gods.

The significance of the title of the book is found in the last paragraph, where Antony says, "Our hardest task will be to guard our love from the world of men" (*AM*, 574)—although Katha had first warned him: " 'Always hide happiness, Antony. Don't let them see we are lovers. Don't. It isn't that I don't hate concealment or that I'm not proud you love me, but once people know, they always try to kill happiness' " (*AM*, 128). Some justice exists in these comments, as the experiences of Antony and Katha indicate; and a full statement of the axiom is found very early in the story in a reference to Antony's childhood:

Even then he saw that what for him were the essential, all-important experiences could be revealed to others only at his peril. You might take life carelessly from the outside, as they did at school; for you might come to it in the abstract intellectual way, like his father; or you might make it a spiritualized abstraction, like his mother; but if you went to life with all your senses open, with your body as well as your mind, with your own fresh feelings instead of abstract laid-down ones, then indeed all men were your enemies. (*AM*, 31)

This principle is important in Aldington's writings, and it can probably be applied to all idealists who refuse to acquiesce to the expectations of those about them. The lawlessness of Antony's ambitions— love without marriage and life without gainful employment—makes it impossible for him to expect the approval of society at large, or to hope for its sympathy when his plans are not fulfilled. It is also doubtful that a man can truly "live with gusto" and achieve a "finer fuller life" by leading a wholly unproductive existence. At any rate, the author himself never lived such a life. Life, of course, is just beginning again for Antony; and there is still much time for him to determine the way he really wishes to spend it. He has abandoned those pursuits which he finds useless and ungratifying, and he now has the opportunity to do whatever pleases him.

All Men Are Enemies is Aldington's best novel after *Death of A Hero*. It is a very touching love story with an arresting plot, vivid scenic description, and well-developed characterization; but it is limited by its expression of a conception of life which dismisses the problems of society at large as the hero seeks happiness and self-fulfillment with the woman he loves.

CHAPTER 7

The "Finer Fuller Life"

A LDINGTON never loses sight of his conception of a "finer fuller life"; for, though *All Men Are Enemies* is the ultimate expression of his vision of romantic idealism, his subsequent heroes and heroines are also preoccupied with the problem of finding personal satisfaction within or beyond the social framework which would limit their privileges. The author, moreover, holds to the principle that a person must first know pain before he can appreciate happiness; for it is necessary for one to understand reality if he is to safeguard his ideals. Antony, in *All Men Are Enemies*, is the man Aldington wished to be—an idealist who has adjusted himself to the realities of life, who is capable of enjoying the benefits of two worlds without becoming a martyr to either. For the woman of the author's middle-class background, the matter is not so simple: she lacks the freedom and opportunities of the man and often finds her happiness dependent upon the whims of men. If she is beautiful and wealthy—and wealth is the more essential of the two qualities—she may escape from social pressures and live more or less as she chooses. If she is both plain and poor, like Georgie in *The Colonel's Daughter*, she may be deprived of the most humble of woman's ambitions, the desire for a home of her own with a husband and children. The woman's life becomes even more difficult when she tries to obtain more than this.

I Women Must Work

In *Women Must Work*, (1934),[1] Etta Morison is handicapped by beauty unaccompanied by wealth. Whereas Georgie Smithers asks for nothing more than a chance to live the life which her society expects of her, Etta, who is more ambitious and enterprising, is also more sensitive and intelligent; she also possesses deeper emotional needs which must be satisfied. The author includes details in her childhood which are similar to those of his own. Etta's Dortborough parallels the descriptions of Dover in Aldington's autobiography and in his poem "Childhood," and she hates the dreary town with the same fervor which Aldington expresses in his poem. Her childhood memories are overshadowed by disagreeable experiences. She attends a private institution under the supervision of two elderly sisters, whose description appears to owe something to Thackeray's account of the Misses Pinkerton in *Vanity Fair*. To intensify Etta's misery at home and at school, moreover, Aldington does not permit her to enjoy the regular holidays in the country which made his own early years more pleasant.

Etta's early childhood is given brief treatment in a prologue; almost nothing is said of her later childhood and adolescence; and the rest of the novel is concerned with her life from the age of nineteen onwards. Etta, who is depressed by the fear that she will never escape the town which she hates, either by marrying or by remaining with her parents, often remarks, "I would rather die than live all my life in Dortborough" (*W*, 23). Her struggles for independence are both tragic and amusing; and touches of Dickensian humor and pathos appear without excessive caricature or sentimentality in the description of her Sunday afternoon beside the Morison hearth, her tea party at the Lawsons, her London office in which she works, her first employer's antics, and the rooming house of Miss Millingham. The same Dickensian elements are present in the next part of the novel, which deals with Etta's life in the Lawson household and with her activities during World War I; and her devotion and gratitude toward Ada Lawson, her second employer, are almost worthy of a Dickensian heroine. Etta's unsuccessful attempt after the war to manage a small farm recalls the labors of the author at his Hermitage cottage in Berkshire, the local color of the English countryside, and the dialect and humor of its inhabitants. The unexpected reunion there between Ralph (a former lover) and Etta, however, is nineteenth-century melodrama, as is her dismissal of him; but this section has the virtue of being brief.

As C. P. Snow points out, Etta's "life is shown in terms of the 'tragedy of material success,' 'the tragedy of the emancipated woman of the war epoch.' "[2] Nonetheless, the heroine is a puzzling character; and her tragedy may be explained as the waste of a strong will and a good intelligence upon unworthy objects, for she has no clearly formulated ideals or sense of direction. She is a sensitive

woman with an artistic temperament who gradually becomes
"hardened"—this word is repeated again and again throughout the
story—against other people and against the promptings of her own
natural and better feelings. Before she is nineteen, Etta gives up a
possible career in music because her teacher tells her that she does
not have the talent to be a "first-class" pianist (W, 22), but she then
spends years struggling to succeed in other pursuits which she finds
less enjoyable and, for a long time, unpromising and unrewarding.
In addition, her poverty during her first months in London so cor-
rupts her former honesty and generosity that she becomes a selfish,
scheming woman whose chief preoccupation in life is to earn and
save money, an unthinkable ambition for Aldington's male heroes.
She becomes the type of person—the ruthless commercialist—for
whom Aldington elsewhere shows contempt. The author has
learned, however, to criticize society and its institutions without
direct commentary, conveying his meaning by merely telling a
story, and no one can miss the irony of Etta's life. While Etta tries to
excuse her aims by insisting that she needs the money for Anne, her
illegitimate daughter, the relationship between her and her daughter indicates that the mother is not acting in the best interests of the
child.

The welfare of Etta's daughter introduces a problem regarding
the attitudes of Aldington's "enlightened" women toward sex and
marriage, but to discuss the moral aspects of this situation is unnecessary, since the practical difficulties encountered by these
women are sufficient to question the wisdom of their behavior. In
Death of a Hero, for example, Elizabeth does not have difficulty
practicing free love until she suspects that she is pregnant, and she
then abandons her ideal until she is certain of safety and respectability. Etta is more daring—and perhaps more foolish—for she delib-
erately has an illegitimate child, only to discover that she must let
her friend Vera create the fiction of a soldier-husband who has been
killed in the war. She is "Mrs." Morison when the baby is born in
the country; and, when she returns to London, she finds she must
maintain the fiction, since even the less scrupulous world of business demands a pretense of respectability.

Women Must Work reveals the irony of Etta's life and indicates
that her happiness will probably be short-lived. By restricting himself to an account of Etta's point of view, Aldington artfully conceals
much of the dissatisfaction with Etta expressed by the other charac-

ters, especially by Anne and Maurice, but the hints are too obvious to be overlooked. Etta is troubled by Anne's lack of affection for her, but she has so forgotten the experiences of her own childhood that she is not aware of the causes. Her job prevents her from being a real mother to Anne, whose care is left to a nurse, a drawback to Etta's belief that a woman is capable of rearing a child properly without a father. Her lover, Maurice, whom she later marries, provides a partial solution to the problem by giving Anne the affection she needs, and Anne is enchanted by his attention and permissiveness. They are genuinely fond of each other, but one suspects that they are motivated by the unconscious desire for an ally against Etta, who is determined to dominate both of them.

From the start, Etta manages Maurice's life for him; and she enjoys this reversal of the usual relationship between a man and a woman. It is less certain that Maurice is as happy with his own role; he never argues with Etta, nor does he ever complain to her. He senses that she loves him because he allows her to have her way, and he is too shrewd to risk giving up the luxury of being kept by a beautiful woman who encourages his ambitions as an artist, though he is troubled by her insistence that he produce more work of commercial value. Not content with gaining her own independence and becoming the equal of any man, Etta is corrupted by her sense of power and is unable to rest until she can exercise her superiority over a man. Though it is tragic that many of the women of Etta's generation suffered because of their inferior position in society, the reversal of the situation in *Women Must Work* does not suggest a more felicitous alternative. It is apparent that Etta has not solved her problems, nor can she hope to do so unless she becomes less selfish and more sympathetic in her relationships with others. The theme of the novel appears to be that women must work for equality with men but not for superiority over them, or other women, if they are to be happy and have meaningful lives.

II Very Heaven

So far, Aldington's novels have dealt chiefly with men and women of his own time, with only incidental references to those who were too young to be involved in the war. The most conspicuous of the characters who have not reached adulthood before the end of the war are Margy Stuart in *The Colonel's Daughter,* Julian in *All Men Are Enemies,* and Maurice in *Women Must Work.* Margy is able to enjoy the gaiety of postwar life without bitter memories; Julian is chagrined by the feeling that he has missed the great event of his time; and Maurice is at least temporarily complacent in his marriage to a selfish older woman who desires him as a compensation for her own sufferings. These youths of the postwar era were born too late to have their early adult lives shattered by the war and too soon to be troubled by the approach of World War II.

Chris Heylin in *Very Heaven* (1937)[3] is a member of the new prewar generation, that is about to face the agony of the second war. No specific dates or historical events are mentioned in the book, apart from the comment that "this is the fourth decade of the twentieth century" (*VH*, 311), but repeated allusions occur to the advancing war. While the threat of war is not the most urgent problem confronting Chris throughout the novel, it has the effect of disturbing his peace of mind and of poisoning his feelings as he attempts to adjust to the unexpected reverses of his life. As C. P. Snow remarks, "Chris Heylin is a symbolic figure, twenty years younger than George Winterbourne, but of the same kind. He stands for the intelligent and sensitive young in a period of suspense, decay, and the loss of hope."[4]

The title of the novel is taken from Book 11 of *The Prelude* where Wordsworth is rhapsodizing about the French Revolution: "Bliss was it in that dawn to be alive, But to be young was very heaven!" (lines 108–9). Though there is irony in Aldington's choice of a title, Chris's hopes of happiness always prove stronger than his feelings of despair; and his youthful ecstasy is not destroyed by the series of calamities that befall him during the six months with which the book deals. As in the case of Aldington's other heroes and heroines, Chris is handicapped by his poverty; for the sudden loss of the Heylin fortune at the beginning of the story initiates a chain of events which leads the family to additional misery and ruin. The situation is both pathetic and repugnant; for, having hitherto spent their lives in the security and comfort of an inherited income, Chris's parents are unable to reconcile the ideals of the past century with the realities of the present one. The cant and humbug of the Victorian period have lingered into a time when they have become bizarre anachronisms. Absurd as their antics may be, Chris's father and mother mean well, but they show lack of imagination and good sense in meeting the crisis. They can think of no other solution to the problem, now that they are insolvent, than to arrange hasty marriages for their children to persons who have money; how unsuitable the partners may be does not concern the parents.

Chris is to be admired for his candor. He is absolutely honest with himself and others, detesting all sham and hypocrisy. His only fault is that he frequently offends others by his lack of tact. Chris cannot be criticized for rebelling against his parents, for he finds himself in the position of assuming the responsibilities of his incompetent elders by default. His handicaps and frustrations are enough to tax the patience of any intelligent young man, and his subsequent feelings of regret for his tactlessness are evidence that he is gradually becoming more mature. Nevertheless, he is often unnecessarily spiteful in expressing his views. In fact, he causes his father's death by writing him a savage letter blaming him for his sister Julie's misfortunes. His kindness to Gwen (his first mistress), Julie, and his mother, moreover, follows calamities which might have been less painful had he shown more understanding beforehand. Though Chris is handsome, his straightforward and unflattering manner with women repels rather than attracts them. Even Martha Wickersham (his second mistress) is slightly repelled by Chris's cynicism and his habit of overintellectualizing his feelings. She never quarrels with him, but she prefers to avoid serious discussions and to encourage the gay and romantic side of his nature.

The hero might have had fewer difficulties had he shown as much delicacy in his dealings with others, such as Winthrop Chepston, as he does in his love affair with Martha. The most important of his potential benefactors is Chepston, his former tutor at the university. While he is understandably irritated by Chepston's pretensions of superior knowledge and wisdom, Chris is guilty of ingratitude by not concealing his contempt for the older man's views. Many of Chris's remarks are gratuitously sarcastic and contentious, and they arouse doubts concerning his supposed sensitivity, since he does not appear to be aware of the effect of his words upon Chepston.

By the end of the novel, Chris's combined disappointments are almost more than he can bear, and he almost commits suicide by flinging himself from a high cliff into the sea:

As he stood there hesitating before the final leap and profoundly moved by this vast elemental splendour, one of the first butterflies of spring, a delicate sulphur yellow, flickered past him.

A downward eddy of air caught the fragile thing and dragged it down towards the bruising rocks and engulfing sea. Chris watched it with intense anxiety. The insect fluttered helplessly, was drawn down out of sight, just missing a sharp rock-edge, and then reappeared floating on light wings out to sea. . . . It flickered higher, circled round, and then was caught in another eddy which carried it safely back to land. Chris watched its dancing flight until it disappeared in the more brilliant yellow of a flowering broom plant. (VH, 335)

Chris asks himself, "If I care so much for the death of so slight a creature, why so little for my own?" (VH, 335). He has failed in everything which he has attempted thus far; he has lost the affection of everyone except Martha; but he is determined to make "one more effort" (VH, 341). Thus, in spite of the gloom and pessimism which is found throughout the book—as Chris's fortunes steadily decline—the story ends on a hopeful and positive note; and Aldington reaffirms the "goodness of life" (VH, 337, 342) which he expressed earlier in the final portion of his poem Life Quest.

III   Seven Against Reeves

In Seven Against Reeves (1938),[5] Aldington ignores the approaching second great war and the problems of the young men and women who are about to be drawn into it. He turns instead to a lighthearted satire of human follies in an England and Europe that are still at peace. In comparison with Aldington's other novels, Seven Against Reeves is remarkable, as C. P. Snow observes, for "its sustained fun and high spirits."[6] Subtitled A Comedy-Farce, the book reveals an adroit wit and a pleasant sense of humor which combine to produce a highly entertaining story of a quasi-picaresque nature.

John Mason Reeves is the antithesis of Richard Aldington, but the author treats him so sympathetically that he becomes a lovable character. At the age of fifty, Reeves has just retired from a successful business career in the city of London. For years, the plump, balding, bespectacled gentleman has looked forward to this moment; but he has been so busy making money and caring for his family that he has neglected to plan for his retirement. The story opens on the morning of the first day of his new life, which is related in an amusing manner, and the fun and humor increase as the story continues; for Reeves does not know what to do with the time which he now has on his hands, and he soon becomes bored with himself and a nuisance to his wife and servants who are not accustomed to having him around the house all day.

Mrs. Reeves, who is a social climber, mistakenly imagines that her husband will enjoy the company of the "right people" now that he has the money and leisure to do as he pleases. There are Dickensian elements in the description of the people who attend the cocktail party which she arranges for him:

> Mr Reeves found himself shaking hands first with a middle-aged spinsterish sort of schoolmarm, whose face irresistibly reminded him of twopenn'orth of fried fish and chips; and then with a fat pompous man, who for some reason made Mr Reeves think of a perambulating pork chop. The pork chop was not quite exact, for Mr Robert possessed a tomato-juice complexion which suggested buckets of Scotch, taken internally. He had staring blue eyes which switched about furtively and a ponderous immobility of carriage which suggested a vast pig immobilized in mud. His little sky-pointing snout led Mr Reeves to expect a series of squeals instead of human speech. (*SR*, 40)

Other persons at the party are described in the same humorous manner: Reeves talks to "waggling young men who painted and stumpy young men who danced and hoarse young men who sang" (*SR*, 44–45); and he is "much shocked by a flat-chested young woman in a pink frock," who gives him "an expert lecture on modern methods of birth control," and he is horrified by the political ideas which are current at the party.

The party offers a preview of the *beau monde* into which Reeves is about to step, in conformance with his wife's wishes and against his own inclinations. He becomes increasingly disturbed by her extravagances and social aspirations, which are beginning to cost him a great deal of money, especially during their weekend with the Faddiman-Fishes, who elicit a large donation to help them subsidize a young composer "to write a genuine British opera" (*SR*, 111). The young composer's bizarre piano recital at the Faddiman-Fishes is reminiscent of the recital which Aldington describes in "Nobody's Baby," but the satire here and elsewhere in the novel does not appear to focus upon individuals taken from real life, and the characters may be regarded as fanciful composites of people whom the author has known. The weekend is filled with amusing characters and dialogue, but the most amusing part of the episode is the dialogue between Reeves and two musicologists from the university on "the moral meaning of pigsties" (SR, 134), which takes place when he encounters the gentlemen during a stroll around the Faddiman-Fish estate.

A crisis finally occurs when Reeves is accused by his wife of having an affair with another woman; and, after he manages to pacify her by promising to take her abroad, they depart for Venice. In an account which reflects Aldington's entertaining conversations with Norman Douglas and Pino Orioli, some English and Italian acquaintances get Reeves drunk in an attempt to persuade him to buy shares in a new literary review, and he is compelled to flee to Cannes to avoid further pestering by such people. After a series of misadventures involving his wife, son, and daughter, Reeves returns to England with his family; he elicits a promise from his wife to give up her social climbing; and he announces that he is going back to work "to pay off these bills and get a little peace and quiet and decent companionship again" (SR, 305).

The story has a happy ending. Though Reeves and his family get into some terrible scrapes, his amiability and good sense always manage to put things right and to show the others the absurdity of their follies and melodramatic behavior. In addition to Reeves and his wife, Aldington produces some other memorable characters in the book—Hawksneetch, the Roberts, and the Faddiman-Fishes—whose speech and behavior never cease to amuse the reader.

IV Rejected Guest

Rejected Guest (1939)[7] returns to the youth who are facing another world war. David Norris is the illegitimate child of a baronet's son and a rent-collector's daughter. Though more than a fourth of the novel is devoted to the circumstances of David's birth and childhood, the plot moves quickly and the narrative is interspersed with well-chosen bits of dialogue which give verve to the story. When David's father is killed in the war, his mother abandons the child to the care of her parents. A bright child, David struggles to obtain an education in spite of the poverty of his grandparents who eventually die and leave him with a small but inadequate inheritance with which to complete his studies at the university. David's town of Ruxton resembles Etta's Dortborough in Women Must Work, and both towns again recall Aldington's account of Dover in his autobiography and "Childhood" poem. David's sentiments concerning dreary English towns are similar to Etta's when he is overcome by "the sickening fear . . . that he might have to live all his life in Ruxton and never know the world" (*RG*, 49). The image of the child as a captive moth, previously mentioned in the discussion of the "Childhood" poem, also reappears in an early passage of *Rejected Guest* (*RG*, 21–22). As in the case of his childhood experiences, David's first two years in London are presented to the reader in a form which is largely narrative; for little dialogue occurs between the characters.

In the remaining sixty percent of the novel which deals with the hero's adventures, the author strikes something of a balance between passages of narrative and dialogue; and the episode begins with David's appeal to his paternal grandfather, Sir Thomas Danby. David is an exact image of his father, and the meeting between Sir Thomas and David is very melodramatic, as are some of the scenes which follow. The author is aware of this, for he has someone remark afterward about the scenes, "The long-lost heir! It's like a nineteenth-century novel"; and he has David reply, "Rather like a Waverley novel" (*RG*, 164). In addition, David is portrayed as something of a combination of Oliver Twist and David Copperfield in a few of the subsequent scenes, though any resemblance of the plot and characters to those of Scott and Dickens is apparent only in a small segment of the book; and Aldington is to be criticized less for this than for his tendency to present David—here and throughout the remainder of the story—as a sentimental and obstinate fool. Chris Heylin in *Very Heaven* falls from wealth into poverty, whereas David rises from poverty to temporary opulence, but both are guilty of ingratitude to their would-be benefactors and suffer accordingly. Like Chris, David is supposedly endowed with a good mind and a sensitive nature, but he often behaves in such a way as to make the reader doubt that he has either of these qualities.

David's *annus mirabilis* begins when he receives a liberal allowance from his grandfather. He departs for the French Riviera with Johnny Martindale, his father's closest friend, who has appointed himself David's guardian. Martindale, a man of the author's own generation, is the most interesting and adequately developed character in the story—an exuberant "man of the world" (*RG*, 163) with a keen wit and a good-natured cynicism toward life. Aldington's description of the Mediterranean region is at least equal to that found in *All Men Are Enemies*. His account of David's romance with

Diana Rockingham, along with the description of the lovely scenery which serves as a background for their passion, is the best part of the novel. An idyllic spring passes on to an even more idyllic summer as they drift about the Mediterranean on Diana's tiny yacht. After David becomes a good sailor, he purchases a larger boat and plans to spend his life sailing around the world with Diana. For a time, it seems that they will actually succeed in sailing past the Strait of Gibraltar—into the sunset and away from the advancing war. Aldington, however, is too much of a realist to permit them to do so, and David's future remains as uncertain as Chris Heylin's in *Very Heaven*.

V   The Romance of Casanova

Rejected Guest is the last one of Aldington's novels about twentieth-century English society. The reason for his sudden abandonment of a career as a novelist is explained in his autobiography: "For more than ten years I had been engaged on a series of more or less satirical novels, giving my views of the period which was called 'post-war' but was in fact merely a long armistice. After listening to Mr. Chamberlain's speech over the radio on the morning of 3 September 1939, I threw the novel I was writing into the waste basket. It would be absurd to denounce calamity; ignoble to satirize a people fighting for their existence."[8] *The Romance of Casanova* (1946),[9] published seven years later, provides a sort of anticlimax to Aldington's efforts to write fiction since the author has ceased to satirize his own world and has turned instead to a story of high adventure based on the *Mémoirs* of the famous Venetian gentleman. As an historical novel, however, the book deserves an excellent rating, for Aldington infuses it with a vitality that reflects his own many travels to Venice and other parts of Italy. His personal acquaintance with the country and the people—their language, their customs, and their history—brings to life a bygone era and makes it seem less remote from the world today.

The novel starts with a prologue in which the aged Casanova, longing for his youth and for a last fling, learns of the fall of the thousand-year-old Venetian Republic, whose vengeance he has feared if he reveals the entire truth of his life, for his doing so would mean the betrayal of state secrets. Encouraged by his safety now, he accepts the challenge of another old gentleman to produce evidence that he, Giacomo Casanova, was "at least once" really "in love and was loved" for his "own sake" (*R*, 23). The tale is filled with suspense as the young Casanova pursues a beautiful and mysterious young woman, is at the same time engaging in amusing love affairs with other ladies, and is always one step ahead of their outraged husbands or guardians. Henriette, the pursued one, is very different from the other women whom Casanova has known, and a less easy prey to his charm, but she too falls in love with him. Though she always forgives him for his faults and is ready to take any risk for his sake, the intrigues of hostile governments, the jealousy of a jilted marchesa, and the inability of Casanova to remain faithful to any woman eventually destroy their hope of a life together.

Apart from the plot, much of the appeal of the novel is found in the author's attention to details in his description of scenes and characters. Aldington's wit and humor also enrich the story; they create an atmosphere of gaiety and frivolity befitting a man such as Casanova. Some passages reveal a more solemn mood, and the last part of the book is fairly consistent in the seriousness of its tone. But the carnival, with its masks, confetti, chance flirtations, jesting, dining, gaming, and lovemaking creates a delightful picture of eighteenth-century Italian life and makes *The Romance of Casanova* a very entertaining story. While this novel is not one of Aldington's more important ones, it displays a great deal of the craftsmanship found in the other stories and constitutes a considerable achievement for the writer.

CHAPTER 8

The Biographer, Translator, and Critic

IN addition to his poems, novels, and short stories, Aldington has produced many fine essays, translations, and biographies. The majority of his essays and translations were published during the same years that he was writing verse and prose fiction; and, for a long time, they were the principal source of his income and the support of his more creative work. Like many other poets of the twentieth century, Aldington never earned enough from his verse to become a full-time poet, though doing so had been his childhood dream. In fact, his work as a critic and a translator eventually gave him the money and leisure to write his first novel. His success as a novelist, in turn, permitted him to discontinue the other work and to devote his time to writing fiction and long poems.

One can only guess why Aldington abandoned poetry after the publication of *The Crystal World* in 1937. He may have been disappointed in the inadequate monetary reward, but it is more likely that he believed the novel to be his real métier. His reason for giving up a career as a novelist a couple of years later has been mentioned by him: he thought it "absurd" and "ignoble" to continue to satirize a society involved in the tragedy of a second world war. He goes on to say, "For some months I felt that my occupation in life had gone, and that I had better find something else to do."[1] This predicament led to the writing and publication of his autobiography, *Life for Life's Sake*, within the next two years. After this work, Aldington's chief interest was biography, and he published his last two studies only five years before his death.

I *Biographies*

Until 1943, Aldington had written only one important biography, *Voltaire* (1925); but he had later published brief studies of D. H. Lawrence (1927), Remy de Gourmont (1928), and Charles Waterton

(1934). The book about Voltaire is divided into two parts: the life and the works. While it is based upon Aldington's thorough study of Voltaire and his writings, he designed the biography to appeal to the general reader rather than to the scholar: its purpose is "to make a bridge between the mass of existing Voltaire knowledge and the people who would like to know the essence of it, yet have neither time nor desire to make a close study."[2]

In describing this approach to his subject in the biographical part of the book, Aldington modestly admits that he is not attempting "some wholly new interpretation" of Voltaire's "complex and contradictory personality" but is simply trying "to tell what seems to be the truth as clearly as possible."[3] Though he takes care to distinguish between fact and legend, his account of the fascinating events of Voltaire's life is written in the lively and entertaining style which is characteristic of his other work; and his genuine esteem for the man is always apparent. As in his later biographies, Aldington does not hesitate to indicate the faults and weaknesses of his subject, but he emphasizes those qualities which he admires in Voltaire—his wit, his genius, his humanitarianism, his appreciation of art and literature, and, above all, his ability to live his life with gusto. He regards Voltaire as "the master of French light verse"[4] and notes that "the best modern French prose is still the prose of Voltaire."[5] Equally important, in Aldington's opinion, is the observation that Voltaire possesses "a European mind"[6] which is free of any narrow provincialism.

The Duke (1943), a biography of Wellington, is a more ambitious piece of work; a detailed study, it is designed to serve as a definitive biography of a great man. Notwithstanding the many details concerning the duke of Wellington and his milieu, Aldington brings the man himself to life throughout the book. The reader is able to follow the "idle, dreamy, shy" boy,[7] whose only early interest seemed to be his violin, through his initial failures to his brilliant successes on the battlefield. Aldington's appraisal of Wellington's military achievements is also well-supported by documentary evidence and maps of the campaigns. The account of this long and interesting life, moreover, ends with an endearing description of the aged duke's refighting with pillows the Battle of Waterloo with his grandchildren and their friends.

Four English Portraits (1948) appears to be a by-product of *The Duke*; for, as the author says, the book provides "sketches" rather than full-length portraits of four remarkable men in an attempt "to touch four different strata" of English society from 1801 to 1851.[8] "The Grand World of 'Prinney' " is a portrait of George IV, who is depicted as a reasonably good king and as an intelligent, cultured patron of arts and letters. In "The Lustrous World of Young Disraeli," the colorful youth of the great British prime minister is portrayed vividly; and the development of his thoughts and ambitions is skillfully illustrated by extracts from his novels. "The Strange World of Squire Waterton" is another brief sketch of the eccentric country gentleman who is the subject of Aldington's next biography. In the last piece, "The Underworld of Young Dickens," Aldington focuses more upon a criticism of Dickens' work than upon a portrayal of the man and his milieu. Instead of illustrating the personality of the man behind his publications, many quotations from Dickens' writings indicate the genius of their author in describing London slums and streets. Although this essay is a good introduction to the early novels, less than half of it deals directly with young Dickens himself; and, as a result, the reader loses sight of Aldington's aim to present, "through the events of Dickens's childhood," some "dreadful glimpses of the lives of drab and helpless suffering endured by children caught in the ruthless machinery of industrialism."[9]

In 1949, Aldington finally published a full-length portrait, *The Strange Life of Charles Waterton, 1782–1865*, of the eccentric country squire who had interested him for at least seventeen years. The reason for his attraction to "the Squire," as well as to "the Duke," is expressed in the opening paragraph: "Both were men of strong individuality, robust humour, pungent expressions, opinionated, without self-consciousness, detesters of humbug and contemners of idleness." He adds, however, that, while Wellington's "practical genius made him the hero of his age and country, Charles Waterton, by whimsical quirks of character developed by education, became one of its strangest freaks, a holy clown, a kind of ornithological Brother Juniper."[10] Aldington's sympathetic record of the activities and adventures of this most unusual man makes delightful and fascinating reading, and the account is enriched by quotations from Waterton's autobiographical writings.

In the next biography, Aldington writes about a man of his own time, one whom he knew well and admired greatly, D. H. Lawrence. Though Aldington had published briefer studies of Lawrence as early as 1927, his *Portrait of a Genius But . . .* (1950) is the only book in which he gives full treatment to the life of his old friend and onetime colleague in the imagist movement. The author makes no claim to having written a definitive biography—the credit for that must now go to Edward Nehls for his compilation of the three-volume *D. H. Lawrence: A Composite Biography*—but Aldington's book is valuable for the many insights it offers concerning Lawrence's character.

Aldington explains that his choice of title was the result of his discovery, in reviewing books and letters about the man, that "somewhere or other almost everyone used the phrase: 'Of course, Lawrence was a genius, but. . . .' "[11] In this book and elsewhere, Aldington is consistent in his praise of Lawrence's genius, "both in living and in writing."[12] But Aldington is no hero-worshiper. His love and admiration for the man and his work have in no way prevented him from dealing with Lawrence's faults as well as his virtues. The book is all the better because of this objectivity, since Lawrence is presented to the reader as an all-too-human man of flesh and blood—as a genius, but also as a human being with whom the reader can sympathize. The verve and the readability of Aldington's prose style also contribute to the worth of the book, and one can read it almost as one would read a novel. The pace seldom lags, especially in the first part of the book; and the numerous quotations from the writings of Lawrence and others are as skillfully introduced—and are as much an organic part of the whole—as they are in the biography of Waterton. Though Aldington says little about his own personal relations with Lawrence, his intimacy with Lawrence during brief periods is apparent in his sympathetic treatment of his subject throughout the book.

Pinorman (1954) is also a book about men whom Aldington knew intimately, and he explains that the title is "a portmanteau word used by themselves and friends for Pino (Orioli) and Norman (Douglas)."[13] The material is arranged in a loosely chronological manner, and is largely a hodgepodge of miscellaneous information about Douglas, Orioli, and Charles Prentice; but the emphasis is upon Aldington's relationship with these three men. The book begins with a discussion of the menus of the restaurants where he dined with them, and it ends with a personal assessment of Douglas' character.

Aldington's fluent and energetic style sustains the reader's interest throughout the book, but the best passages are those which contain his recollections of the colorful Orioli, whom he describes as a sort of "Boccaccio junior."[14] While he speaks of Orioli and Prentice in the warmest and most affectionate terms, he is rather severe in his portrait of Douglas—far more so than he was in his autobiography nearly fifteen years earlier, where one hardly suspects that he felt any strong disapproval of Douglas. Although Aldington's admiration for Douglas and his work is present in *Pinorman*, it is overshadowed by unfavorable criticism of both. Aldington is not vitriolic in speaking of Douglas, but he stresses the man's malice, pettiness, and depravity—almost in a tone of sadness or disappointment as he does so. Even though he denies, in a prefatory note, that the book is "an attempted biography," one wonders if it is fair to offer even tentative judgments of a man without making a more thorough study of his life, as the author may have planned to do at one time. Aldington's most valuable contributions are his personal recollections of Douglas rather than his cursory survey of the man's life and character.

In the meantime, following the publication of his biography of D. H. Lawrence in 1950, Aldington had been preparing a much more important work than *Pinorman*. This important new book was *Lawrence of Arabia: A Biographical Enquiry* (1955). As in the case of the study of Wellington, his "lack of enthusiasm for military heroes" was partly responsible for his hesitance in writing a book about Thomas Edward Lawrence.[15] The book on Lawrence was suggested to Aldington by his friend and private secretary, Alister Kershaw, who prevailed upon him to undertake the study; and Aldington's discoveries about Lawrence surprised the author as much as anyone else. Another friend, Henry Williamson, notes that he has "many letters from Richard, the majority of them discussing . . . a biography of T. E. Lawrence," and that he "saw how the book was to progress—the letters from expressing wonder eventually became scornful and then dismissive of the 'hero.' "[16] Aldington's own claims for his achievement are very modest: "I do not pretend to have written the definitive biography of Lawrence, nor is this in any sense a final portrait of the man. Much of the evidence that is necessary for such a task is still not available."[17] Be that as it may, the book presents the results of a tremendous amount of research and scholarship, and no one can now undertake a serious study of T. E. Lawrence without consulting the author's numerous sources of information.

Aldington's integrity as a biographer is well illustrated throughout the book, for he takes scrupulous care that any statement of fact is adequately supported by irrefutable evidence, and he always shows skepticism concerning any matter for which sufficient proof does not exist. In doing so, he has proven beyond any shadow of reasonable doubt that T. E. Lawrence was not the great man or hero that the public had believed him to be; that, in fact, Lawrence was an inveterate exaggerator who had a genius for self-advertisement and an amazing ability to deceive and mystify others; that his success may be attributed not only to his own ambitions but to the personal aspirations and political motives of various Englishmen and Americans; and that the first and most important of these personages was the American correspondent Lowell Thomas. Furthermore, as Aldington demonstrates time and time again, the "edifice" of the legend "shows a fairly solid front to the uncritical reader but once it has been examined it is shown to be an inverted pyramid at the base of which stands Lawrence himself on whom the legend rests."[18] Not only did Lawrence create most of the legend with its multifarious details, but he helped to perpetuate it not only by writing his *Seven Pillars of Wisdom* (which Lawrence wrote as a true documentary, but which Aldington has shown to be "a work of quasi-fiction rather than history")[19] but also by his collaboration with Lowell Thomas in producing the immensely popular film-lecture and book *(With Lawrence in Arabia)*. He also collaborated with Robert Graves and Liddell Hart on their biographies of him.[20]

Aldington traces the story of Lawrence's ancestry, life, and exploits in great detail. In the first part of the book he deals with the man's life up to the outbreak of World War I, by which time Lawrence's proclivity for aggrandizing himself and his achievements has been well established. The second part follows Lawrence's activities during the war in which his opportunities to glorify himself and his deeds finally found full scope. Aldington does not deny the fact that Lawrence was a man of great nerve, courage, and energy. He indicates only that Lawrence was an incompetent soldier; that he was never the actual leader of large Arab forces; and that his military accomplishments, as well as those of the Arabs in general, were comparatively insignificant. The author also demonstrates that Lawrence never lost an opportunity for making a failure appear to be a triumph or for claiming an honor which did not rightfully belong to him. In the third part of his biographical enquiry, Aldington shows how Lowell Thomas helped Lawrence publicize a legend which the world might otherwise have never known, and how the half-truths continued to gain support and further embellishment through the offices of uncritical hagiographers to whom Aldington refers collectively as the "Lawrence Bureau."[21] While it is made clear that Lawrence indeed had excellent chances for a diplomatic career after the war, his claim that he was offered the posts of home defence and high commissioner for Egypt is shown to be nothing but a fiction which he created himself.

Lawrence of Arabia created such a furor in England and America that Aldington was vehemently denounced for his achievement and was boycotted by the press, the book publishers, and the public at large. This reaction was followed by the silence of the critics, most of whom refused to speak of him or of his work—except in disparaging terms.[22] Though many people were undoubtedly dismayed by Aldington's thorough and scholarly debunking of their hero, his bitterest enemies probably came from the ranks of those who, in his book, had been duped by T. E Lawrence's fictions and half-truths. The book is filled with names of those whom Lawrence deceived and prevailed upon to realize his ambitions, and many were persons of the greatest importance in the British political, military, and literary world. Many of these persons, moreover, were still alive when the book appeared. Not all of them, as the author indicates, had fully trusted Lawrence or believed the legend, but few were probably prepared for the shock of Aldington's exposé. A later generation may be able to view the book in a more dispassionate manner.

Undaunted by the attacks upon his Lawrence of Arabia, Aldington published three more biographical studies within the next two years, and these might have been followed by others had his physicians not advised him to avoid such projects.[23] Introduction to Mistral (1956) is a tribute to the Provençal poet, Frédéric Mistral (1830–1914), who won half of the Nobel Prize for literature in 1904. In addition to a sympathetic sketch of the poet's life and milieu, the book offers a sensitive introduction to the poems of Mistral, summaries of his long narrative pieces, and excerpts from his verse which are accompanied by English translations. As for the biographical work Frauds (1957), it is a miscellany that presents some of the most celebrated frauds and impostors who have gained notoriety in England since the late fifteenth century; and its charm is to be found in the wry humor and ironic wit which permeate the pages.

Portrait of a Rebel: The Life and Works of Robert Louis Stevenson (1957) focuses upon the subject's life as one of rebellion against a narrow religious background, a domineering father, and the exigencies forced upon him by poor health. Throughout the book, Aldington emphasizes the man's courage and determination to lead his own life in a profession of his own choosing. In an effort to draw valid conclusions concerning Stevenson's character, he presents a critical examination of apocryphal data, autobiographical material, and statements by the man's biographers and hagiographers. He also introduces many quotations from Stevenson's writings and compares his letters with those of others. Above all, he tries to reconcile the romance and reality of Stevenson's life, and indicates that the charm of that life is to be found in the writings.

II *Translations*

During Aldington's lifetime, he produced some twenty-nine volumes of translations. Most of these were published in both England and America between the years 1915 and 1932 when he was dependent upon such work as a major source of income. The majority are from French literature, and they include translations from Old French of the *langue d'oïl* and the *langue d'oc*. Some of Aldington's earliest translations are from ancient Greek poetry—the verse of Anyte of Tegea, Meleager of Gadara, and imitators of Anacreon of Teos. Along with his versions of Latin poems of the Renaissance, they are all contained in the small volume called *Medallions in Clay* (1921). Many of the pieces are very short—some of them only epigrams—but all embody the lyrical qualities which Aldington has tried to recapture in his own poetry. He has selected poems which reveal a passion for the beauty of nature and lovely women, for the pleasures of life and the sorrows of death; and the translations are the result of a labor of love in which he feels an awareness of the personalities of the poets themselves, "trying to re-think their thoughts, to re-live their emotions."[24] The pieces are rendered in prose, but the rhythms often approach those of free verse. They are filled with the living myth which is reflected in the "Greek dream" of Aldington's own early poems.

Thomas McGreevy praises *Medallions in Clay* and *Fifty Romance*

Lyric Poems (1928) for "some exquisite renderings of exquisite origi-
nals."[25] *Fifty Romance Lyric Poems*—a selection of short verses
composed by French, Provençal, and Italian poets from the end of
the eleventh century to the middle of the seventeenth century—
includes well-known poets such as Villon, Marot, Ronsard, Bellay,
Petrarch, Boccaccio, Boiardo, Tasso, Marini, as well as many who
are less famous, and a few anonymous pieces. The original poems
and Aldington's graceful prose translations are on pages facing each
other, a great advantage to those readers who wish to compare the
two versions or simply enjoy the poems in the languages in which
they were first composed. *The Garland of Months* (1917), later published with illustrations and an introduction as *A Wreath for San
Gemignano* (1945), is again a prose translation—this time, of a series
of fourteen sonnets by the late thirteenth-century Italian poet Folgore Da San Gemignano. As one critic points out, Aldington's versions "are pleasant, and convey the literal meaning of the original,"
and he adds that, "To perceive the advantages of the prose render-
ing over an attempt to use the sonnet form in translation, one might
compare the present work with Rossetti's labored reconstructions of
the same poems in his 'Early Italian Poets.' "[26]

Aldington's translation of Voltaire's *Candide* (1927) has been reprinted a number of times over the years, including illustrated editions issued in 1928, 1936, and 1959; and it would be difficult to find
a better version of this masterpiece. The same may be said of his
translation of Boccaccio's *Decameron* (1930), which has also undergone successive reprintings. One has only to compare it with earlier
translations to note that the style has a natural quality that is more
pleasing to modern tastes, for Aldington retains a quaint medieval
flavor without employing many of the archaisms or the unnecessarily complicated sentence structures which encumber other versions.

Among Aldington's other fine translations is *French Comedies of
the XVIIIth Century* (1923), which begins with an excellent introduction to eighteenth-century French comedy. *Voyages to the
Moon and the Sun* (1923) by Cyrano de Bergerac is also preceded by
a very good introduction to the legend, life, and works of the author;
and Aldington shows much skill in handling a pair of satirical fantasies which combine lively narrative with dull exposition. Since
Aldington's skill is equally evident in his translation of *Sturly* (1924)
by Pierre Custot, it seems odd that this work is not better known. It
is a novel of sorts, but the characters are sea creatures who have the

power of human speech. Most fascinating, however, is the remarkably vivid picture of deep-sea life as seen through the eyes of a man who has studied it closely. The accuracy of Aldington's translation is reflected in the praise which he received from both the author and the critic in *Mercure de France* who has called his version *"un véritable tour de force."*[27]

III *Criticism and Miscellaneous Essays*

Alister Kershaw offers the following comments at the beginning of an introduction to a recently published selection of Aldington's critical work: "If the expression had not somehow become frowsy and a bit absurd, Richard Aldington might be described as preeminently a 'man of letters'—the last, perhaps, who will trouble the jubilant illiteracy of this age of 'blind mouths.' The term would seem to be appropriate to Aldington partly because of his lifelong devotion to literature, a devotion which was simultaneously generous and discriminating, and partly because of his own formidable achievements in an exceptionally wide range of genres."[28] There can be no question about Aldington's erudition and virtuosity in describing him as an all-around man of letters. He has not only written poetry and fiction which deserve a place among the minor classics of the twentieth century, but he has published criticism and translations which communicate a sensitive and scholarly appreciation of good books. And this aspect of his career becomes more apparent when one examines his critical essays.

Much of Aldington's criticism is concerned with the literature of France. To a large extent, Aldington was a self-educated man who had taught himself to read French at the age of sixteen in order to share a friend's appreciation for such poets as Ronsard and Chénier.[29] Following his discharge from the army in 1919, he contributed articles on contemporary French literature to the *Anglo-French Review* and served as critic of French literature for *The Times Literary Supplement*. The scholarship demanded by *The Times* makes his success seem all the more remarkable. As he describes his experience,

At a moment's notice I had to be prepared to turn out a more or less adequate article on any book or author from the *Chanson de Roland* to the latest Dadaiste freak. It was like holding a chair in French literature, with this difference, that, instead of talking to youngsters who knew less than I

did, I had to put my views into print to be scanned by thousands of educated people, including a number of hawkeyed and censorious experts. *The
Times* itself was severe about the slightest inaccuracy.[30]

Aldington must have been a very competent critic, for he held the
post for ten years. During this time, he continued his studies in
English, Italian, classical, and French literature; and he even taught
himself to read Old French in the *langue d'oc* and *langue d'oïl*.

The essays in Aldington's first volume of criticism, *Literary
Studies and Reviews* (1924),[31] were originally published as separate
pieces by *The Times* and other periodicals. Of the fourteen of the
twenty-one selections that deal with individual French authors, the
first is about Pierre de Ronsard, one of the poets whom Aldington
had read when he was only sixteen. Beginning with an account of
Ronsard's reputation among his contemporaries and later critics, the
essay discusses the poet's work in terms of the literary aims and
achievements of French, English, and Italian writers of the sixteenth century; and Aldington indicates Ronsard's debt to the past
and his superiority to some of his denigrators in the seventeenth and
eighteenth centuries. Aldington then compares Ronsard's poetry
with Spenser's and calls attention to those lyrics of the French poet
which he feels are equal to some of the best written by the Eliza-
bethans.

A number of other essays conform to much the same format.
Aldington first discusses the man's work relative to its place in European literary history and then discusses the qualities which have
given certain pieces an enduring value and an appeal to the modern
reader. Though he is not addressing an audience of scholars, he
assumes that his readers are educated and that they have a reading
knowledge of French, as well as of Latin and Italian; for he recom-
mends the works in the original language and seldom translates his
numerous quotations.

In his essay on Joachim du Bellay, another important member of
the poetic Pléiade of sixteenth-century France, Aldington acknowledges the poet's lack of originality but shows how the Frenchman
has translated Latin and Italian verse into works of beauty in his own
language. Subsequent essays praise a trio of seventeenth-century
skeptics: Saint-Évremond for his Epicurean charm and delicacy; La
Mothe Le Vayer for his learning and intelligence; Jean Dehénault
for his honesty and poetic talent. The reader who is interested in the

wit and eccentricities of eighteenth-century noblemen, moreover, will be captivated by the sketch of the *Mémoires* of the Prince de Ligne.

As for Aldington's interest in more recent writers, he published an article on Proust prior to his death; and, as Kershaw notes, Aldington was "one of the first to salute the genius of Marcel Proust."[32] In addition to a perceptive recognition of the literary qualities of *À la Récherche du Temps Perdu*, the essay briefly traces the influence of some of Proust's predecessors and compares his work not only with theirs but also with that of contemporary novelists writing in English, such as Joyce. The piece Aldington wrote about Remy de Gourmont preceded a pamphlet about him in 1928, and both essays express a profound admiration for Gourmont as an exceptionally learned and versatile "modern man of letters" (*LS*, 164–66).[33] As in Aldington's other essays, however, he is moderate in his praise; he indicates the weaknesses as well as the virtues of the author's work in an attempt to place it in proper perspective with the literary achievements of other men. Later, in his autobiography, Aldington acknowledges his own debt to Gourmont by referring to him as *"mon vieux ami et maître"*[34] because he "admired his range of interests, his erudition, his French culture, his unbiased judgment, his original point of view, his skepticism, his individualism. He was free from every fanaticism, any form of cant, any subservience either to authority or public opinion. He made a small income by his pen, but he never wrote for money. His integrity, his pure intellectual detachment were never betrayed. . . . His sanity and wisdom were obvious correctives to the disorders and fatuities of the war and post-war years."[35] Some of these ideals which Aldington attempted to imitate in his own writings are the subject of D. Mossop's study, "Un Disciple de Gourmont: Richard Aldington."[36]

In *Literary Studies and Reviews*, which also contains some pieces on English literature, twentieth-century authors are represented by Aldington's early articles on James Joyce and T. S. Eliot. The essay on Eliot, which was first published prior to the appearance of *The Waste Land*, provides some penetrating comments on the emerging literary movements and some insights into Eliot's place among his contemporaries and predecessors. Although the article on Joyce's *Ulysses* was apparently written before the final installment of the novel appeared in its serial publication, and therefore before the first printing as a book in 1922, Aldington's evaluation of the novel in this early review expresses mixed feelings but assesses Joyce's achievement as "remarkable" (*LS*, 192). In the next essay, "The Poet and His Age" Aldington suggests that "the relation of the poet to his age should not be self-conscious, that he should neither reject the actualities, discoveries, the temper of his age, nor should he constitute himself as their interpreter," since these have been errors, respectively, of the romanticists and the futurists (*LS*, 208). He also dismisses the notions that good poetry can be incoherent or addressed to a very limited audience, or that skillful imitation can be substituted for originality, and insists that it is the obligation of the poet to strive to give "the highest pleasure" to the greatest possible number of readers (*LS*, 219). The final item by Aldington in the volume is a prose idyll extolling the "enchantment" of reading Theocritus in the springtime setting of Capri, a fitting conclusion to a somewhat heterogeneous collection of studies which have a common purpose—that of inviting the reader to share the critic's appreciation of good literature.

In *French Studies and Reviews* (1926), the second collection of critical essays by Aldington, the twenty-two selections reprinted are from articles written for periodicals, particularly *The Times Literary Supplement*. Most of the pieces review new studies and edited works which had been recently published by French scholars. The first essay compares two books on French society in the Middle Ages; and, by means of brief quotations, Aldington shows how the two works, taken together, complement each other and serve to round out the picture of medieval life by reconciling the idealism of one with the realism of the other. Aldington's "Early French Texts" discusses the differences between Philippe de Commynes' *Mémoires* and Sir Walter Scott's fictionalized version, *Quentin Durward*, but it also contains a brief but frequently appreciative criticism of other works from the fifteenth century, as well as one from the thirteenth. Aldington completes his treatment of the medieval period with a sensitive evaluation of the poetry of François Villon in terms of the most recent studies and editions of the poet's life and work which were available at the time that the essay was written.

In Aldington's review of two books, *Les Satires Françaises du XVIᵉ Siècle* and *Les Satires Françaises du XVIIᵉ Siècle* (both written jointly by Fernand Fleuret and Louis Perceau), he defends the art of satire as it is employed by many French poets of the sixteenth and seventeenth centuries. He traces its origins and development, criticizes its strengths and weaknesses, and compares its expression with that of English poets of the same periods. In "Four Modern Poets," Aldington examines the verse of Georges Rodenbach, Charles Guérin, Renée Vivien, and Maurice du Plessys. While he notes important differences in their work, he points out that all four express "an unmistakable nostalgia and regret for a lost world, a brooding over vanished beauty."[37] The remainder of the essays in the volume are miscellaneous items which Aldington saw fit for some reason to include among the others.

As in the case of some of Aldington's other books, there have been recent reprints of *French Studies and Reviews* (in 1967) and *Literary Studies and Reviews* (in 1968). This is a hopeful sign of renewed interest in Aldington's criticism, for much of it has permanent value. The most recent publication is *Richard Aldington: Selected Critical Writings, 1928–1960*, edited by Alister Kershaw and with a preface by Harry T. Moore (1970).[38] Moore points out that Aldington is "for the most part an expository critic, leading us along various literary paths and pointing out interesting sights along the way," and that "he sometimes makes rewarding discoveries" (*RA*, x). Kershaw says much the same thing when he observes that Aldington has always taken "the modest view that the function of the critic was to direct attention toward what he considered to be valuable work, to indicate why he considered it valuable, and then, having provided potential readers with an opportunity to share in a new experience, to step out of the picture" (*RA*, xvii).

Kershaw also mentions two important characteristics of Aldington's criticism: "independence of judgment" and "an altogether admirable capacity for generous appreciation." These characteristics enable the critic to succeed "in transmitting his own enthusiasm and thereby awakening in the reader a desire to participate in that intensely felt pleasure" (*RA*, xviii). These traits apply as much to the works which have already been discussed as they do to those in the 1970 volume. In most of his critical work, Aldington combines objectivity with a personal quality which reflects his own feelings and attitudes toward literature. Though he seldom hesitates to point out the faults of any author, he tends to emphasize the features which he admires, and he nearly always does so in such a way that he arouses the reader's interest—or at least his curiosity—concerning the subject. He also has a special talent for persuading the reader to suspend any prejudices until he has examined or reexamined a writer's work.

Selected Critical Writings is comprised of ten of Aldington's essays which cover a period of thirty-two years. The essay about Remy de Gourmont (1928), which has been mentioned in conjunction with an earlier essay about the same author, is, as Moore indicates, "a valuable introduction to this writer" (*RA*, xi). The next two selections are book reviews which were written for the *Sunday Referee* (London), and one of these articles (December 15, 1929) deals with Aldous Huxley's book of essays, *Do What You Will*, which Aldington praises for its expression of "a positive belief in life, a positive enjoyment of life" (*RA*, 20)—a point of view that Aldington has always tried to express in his own writings. The other essay contains a review (June 15, 1930) of Wyndham Lewis' novel, *The Apes of God*, and a reply (June 22, 1930) to Lewis' protests concerning the review. Following these reviews is a reprint of a short pamphlet, *W. Somerset Maugham, An Appreciation* (1939).

The selections also include three introductions which Aldington wrote for newly published editions of the works of earlier authors. In these pieces, as in many of those in *Literary Studies and Reviews* and *French Studies and Reviews*, there is a skillful blending of biographical data and criticism which enhances the appeal to the general reader without obscuring the critical purpose. The introduction to *The Portable Oscar Wilde* (1946) presents the writer's work with respect to the personality, influences, and circumstances which created it. As Moore observes, Aldington's essay "is an extremely fascinating one" which offers "various new perspectives" concerning Wilde's life and work (*RA*, xii). Moore also notes that the introduction to *Walter Pater, Selected Works* (1948) is "excellent"—one of the best pieces, in his estimation, which has ever been written about Pater (*RA*, xii). Despite the meagerness of reliable information about Pater's life, Aldington devotes more than half of this long essay to a penetrating account of the man's development as a writer. In the remainder of the essay, he discusses Pater's thought and style, with emphasis on the continuing value and relevance of his writings. Aldington's introduction to the novels of Jane Austen (1948) is also commended by Moore, who regards it as "very useful because of its observations and rearrangements of perspective" (*RA*, xii).

The last three essays in *Selected Critical Writings* deal with the work of some of Aldington's own friends. One is a eulogy in honor of the memory of Roy Campbell, written first in French soon after the poet's untimely death and printed originally in *Hommage à Roy Campbell* (1958). The item on Lawrence Durrell's *Alexandria Quartet* was written for a review called *Two Cities* (1959), prior to the publication of *Clea*, the concluding novel in the tetralogy. Aldington comments on his own response to the first three books of the Durrell series: "There are not many occasions in life when on reading a new novel one becomes more and more enthusiastic, feeling 'here is a new personality in writing, something pungent and original which will certainly endure.' I experienced that going on for half a century ago with D. H. Lawrence's *Sons and Lovers*, James Joyce's *Ulysses*, and Proust's *Du Côté de chez Swann*. And now again, after a barren period, with *Justine, Balthazar*, and *Mountolive*" (*RA*, 122). In the final essay of this collection, Aldington once again pays tribute to a writer whose work he had admired for many years—D. H. Lawrence. This piece, translated from the introduction written for Frédéric-Jacques Temple's book, *D. H. Lawrence: l'oeuvre et la vie* (1960), appeared first in French, as did the essay on Campbell. Aldington welcomes Temple's book as the first French study to do justice to its subject: "The greatest English writer of this century is at last adequately presented to the French literary public" (*RA*, 131).

One more collection of essays by Aldington should be mentioned, *Artifex: Sketches and Ideas* (1935).[39] The only piece in this group which may be described as genuine literary criticism is the one on D. H. Lawrence which was first published as a pamphlet and later reprinted in the 1936 (American) edition of *Artifex*. Though Aldington admits that the essay is much too brief to serve as an "adequate" discussion of Lawrence's major works, he succeeds very well in offering "a few hints of what seem . . . to be the obvious lines of an intelligent appreciation" (*A*, 209–10).

Aldington calls other items in the book "mere literary echoes," and he also includes some "sketches of people (in one case an animal) half-remembered, half-imagined for purposes of fiction and then not used" (*A*, vi). The remainder of the essays are "articles, though none of them were written for periodicals." The author says that he has "tried to make ideas and travel impressions a little more lively by occasionally bringing in real or imaginary persons, 'scatter-

ing a few flowers' as Voltaire advises us" (A, vi). In "Artifex," the
piece from which the book takes its title, Aldington discusses the
eternal role of the artist—the "servant of the life impulse, maker of
myths, music and images" (A, 10)—as he contemplates the mystery
of the prehistoric cave-paintings of Altamira. Both "Artifex" and "A
Splinter of America" express Aldington's concern for civilization,
which he believes to be dominated by commercial, political, scientific, and religious interests that combine to suppress or pervert
man's aesthetic and humanitarian impulses. In "A Splinter of
America," he deplores the way civilization despoils the natural
beauty of the world as he presents a vivid description of a remote
isle in the West Indies. "Sea Travel" is a continuation of the same
theme, for the author again seeks a means of escape from the pressures and demands of the modern world in order to find serenity by
reestablishing "a harmony" with nature (A, 230). These same
themes and desires that figure so importantly in some of Aldington's
poems, stories, and novels are expressed most fully in *Life Quest,*
for he vows in it "to revere the real holy ones/ Sun Sea and Earth."

CHAPTER 9

The Man of Letters

IN reviewing the many works of Richard Aldington, one is impressed by his variety of genres, subjects, and literary techniques, as well as by his wide range of interests, experiences, feelings, and attitudes. Since Aldington published over a hundred different volumes in his lifetime and wrote introductions to more than a score of others, only his major creative works have been discussed in detail in the preceding chapters; for it is largely in his poetry and fiction that the reader can see the development of his art and ideals.

I *His Imagery*

Aldington was only twenty when he published the poems which launched the imagist movement in 1912. From the start, his verse is characterized by an adoration of natural beauty; and, in his early poems, the myriad deities of nature from the art and myths of ancient Greece provide him with the means by which he can express his sentiments. His paganism is genuine; for, as a general rule, he effectively communicates to the reader his feelings of awe or delight or reverence about his gods, dead gods, about whom he can do little more than lament their passing. He does manage to make them live again in a few poems in which he recaptures the color and animation of scenes from ancient art or from contemporary England.

On the whole, however, Aldington is unable to revivify Greek myth in modern terms, as Yeats, for example, has done. Aside from his use of free verse, he shows little technical and imaginative originality in many of the poems, for the imagery often resembles that of Swinburne and other late nineteenth-century poets, while other pieces appear to be less skillful imitations of the "perfect images" of his wife, H. D. Taken as a group, Aldington's early poems (and even different stanzas of particular poems) indicate that he was unable to produce consistently good images. One has the impression that the

175

imagist credo led him to believe that almost any image would do, as long as it was an image.

The same observation is applicable to Aldington's other early poems, including his imitations of Japanese *haiku*, *haikai*, and *tanka*. Here and there, one notes effective or striking images, but they are comparatively few in number. Aldington continues to pursue the vanishing shades of his Greek dream as he faces the terrible realities of the trenches and battlefields; but while he never ceases to take delight in the beauty of nature, his best war poems are those in which he forgets his dream and gives an objective account of the horrors of modern warfare. By the time one gets to his love poems, Aldington's dream has undergone a significant transformation: the poet is no longer trying to revive the Greek deities of nature in the world about him; he is seeking divine inspiration in his passion for beautiful women, describing their lips, breasts, and bodies as flowers, and endowing his ladies with goddesslike qualities. The poems are characterized by strong passions, and they contain many lovely images. Though some of Aldington's images resemble those of his wife, H. D., they are often equal—and sometimes superior—to hers in vividness and evocative power. Despite the high quality of certain pieces, however, the imagery continues to reflect the influence of poets of the past century, such as Swinburne. Aldington's poems of "exile" offer an account of his recovery from the horrors of the war. At first the poet feels only anguish and despair, but he gradually regains his peace of mind as he recalls his Greek dream of prewar years, while in other poems, he more or less ignores the dream as he appeals to modern attitudes regarding life and death; and these pieces also demonstrate his ability to create striking, original images.

II   *The Poet's Spiritual Progress*

As in the case of Aldington's earlier verse, his long poems are not consistent in their quality; they range from poems of high quality which present many evocative and original images to poems of doubtful merit which present prosaic narratives that are no more "poetic" than the average short story. Aldington's spiritual progress may also be noted in his long poems. Disillusioned with the postwar world, he begins with a farewell to his Greek dream; and he also rejects Christianity—just as he has in his earlier poems—but he is now unable to find anything to take its place. He fears that the poetic spirit within him has been destroyed and that he cannot escape a life of dull mediocrity in a materialistic world. He fails to overcome his loneliness and unhappiness by having a passionate affair with the woman he loves, for she is unable to love him as deeply as he loves her; then he seeks the "perfect" woman—one who can share his feelings to the extent of being unable to live without him—but realizes that such a hope is futile.

Up to this point, Aldington has been unsuccessful in his search for spiritual fulfillment. He has abandoned his Greek dream, rejected Christianity and other organized religions, and relinquished hope of finding the solution in love for other human beings. He sets forth again, as lonely and unhappy as before. As he wanders across Europe, he finds no comfort in contemplating the glories of the past or the present; for the works of men are subject to destruction, and he sees only death, decay, and desolation in the world about him. His quest seems hopeless until he finds inspiration in the more enduring beauty of nature. Aldington has returned to the adoration of natural beauty which is characteristic of his early poems, but he does so with a difference: he no longer relies upon the art and the myths of a dead civilization for the expression of his feelings; he worships nature itself as the life-giving source.

Aldington's quest for life, however, has not come to an end, for he makes an earnest request that his search may continue until he dies. To enjoy his discovery of new life fully, he also needs someone who can share it with him. He does not expect the perfect lovers to be willing to die for each other—it is far better if they can live for each other. Together, the poet and his lady create their own world—a world of beauty inhabited by them alone, since it exists only in the feelings which they share. Though others may smash their secret world, the lovers will recreate it; for, having once known happiness there, they will not be content to accept life in the ordinary world.

III *The Satirist's Sentiments and Ideals*

Aldington's poetic achievement covers a span of twenty-five years, from 1912 to 1937. His career as a novelist was much briefer, for he published his most important prose fiction during a period of ten years, from 1929 to 1939. For this reason, one can hardly anticipate as much technical, intellectual, or spiritual development in the novels as in the poems; but, as may be expected, they reflect some of the sentiments and ideals of the mature poet. Aldington expresses in his novels and short stories his love of nature in the picturesque settings of his narratives, and many scenes evoke images as exquisite as any found in his poems. His characters are happiest when they are able to live in harmony with the natural beauty around them, but their happiness is not complete unless they can share it with a sensitive person of the opposite sex. Their success depends upon their ability to recognize beauty and upon their determination to pursue it despite the opposition of a materialistic society.

The author's satire is aimed at the prejudices and institutions of society—including marriage and the acquisition of wealth and power—which he believes to be inimical to the individual's awareness and pursuit of beauty and happiness, for he feels that the existing familial, social, religious, political, and educational institutions teach hypocrisy and false values. While his satire sometimes takes the form of bitter ridicule and denunciation, Aldington more frequently employs ironic wit and humor in his attempt to expose human follies; but he seldom treats his characters and situations with the cool objectivity which is typical of other twentieth-century English satirists such as Aldous Huxley and Evelyn Waugh.

Aldington's greatest limitation as a novelist is also apparent. He achieves his best results when his protagonist is a man of his own time, class, and temperament, for he is required to do little more than project his own personality and experiences in the story. His main characters are less convincing when they are women, or when they are young men of the next generation. Aldington's young man of the next generation is a prototype of the "angry young man" of an even later generation who is admirable for his candor and integrity, and for his impatience with the incompetence and hypocrisy of his elders; but he often behaves in a manner inconsistent with the personal qualities, intelligence and sensitivity, ascribed to him by displaying obtuseness as well as sensitivity, poor judgment as well as wisdom.

Better overall results are obtained when Aldington satirizes society by means of amusing episodes and caricatures which poke fun at the faults and excesses of both the cultured and the uncultured elements of society. Though the hero shows little change or development throughout this type of novel, he is the more believable because he never breaks character. This observation also applies to Aldington's treatment of character in his historical novel; for, since he is dealing with the famous figure whose traits are already well-established ones, he directs his attention to the plot and to the creation of atmosphere without interfering with the historical concept of the character.

IV *The Translator, Critic, Biographer*

In addition to poetry and fiction, Aldington deserves recognition for his translations, criticism, and biographies. The reader need only compare some of his more important translations with earlier English versions to perceive the superiority of Aldington's. Much of Aldington's literary criticism also has enduring value, and many of his critical essays have been reprinted in recent years. His autobiography is a stimulating account of a career which brought him into contact with many important writers during the first four decades of the twentieth century. His biographies of Voltaire, Mistral, D. H. Lawrence, and the duke of Wellington have been regarded as significant contributions to studies of these men. In all these biographies, he presents lively portraits of his subjects; but he attempts at the same time to separate fact from legend in order to give the reader an accurate understanding of the man and his accomplishments. Despite the merits of his studies of D. H. Lawrence, Norman Douglas, and Lawrence of Arabia, however, he has alienated critics by his lack of hesitance to deal with the men's faults. Ironically, his most original and most thoroughly investigated study—of Lawrence of Arabia—was, as has been observed, the most controversial and the most damaging to his reputation as a writer; but one can only hope that future critics will be able to rise above the controversy and view Aldington's achievement in its proper perspective.

Aldington's works are distinguished by vigor, integrity, and individualism; and the intensity with which he lived his life is reflected in his writings. Though he began his career as an imagist poet, his subsequent writings are the work of a strong individualist whose attitudes and techniques cannot be consistently identified with a particular school or movement. A versatile man of letters, he demonstrated much talent in a variety of literary genres; and his best poems, novels, and stories should endure as minor classics of the twentieth century.

Notes and References

Chapter One

1. References to Aldington's autobiography, *Life for Life's Sake* (New York, 1941), are cited in text as *LL*.
2. Henry Williamson in *Richard Aldington: An Intimate Portrait*, ed. Alister Kershaw and Frédéric-Jacques Temple (Carbondale, Ill., 1965), p. 167.
3. Sir Alec Randall in *Richard Aldington: An Intimate Portrait*, p. 113.
4. Ibid., pp. 112–13.
5. Ibid., pp. 112–15.
6. Ibid., pp. 118–20.
7. Ibid., p. 121.
8. Stanley K. Coffman, Jr., *Imagism: A Chapter for the History of Modern Poetry* (Norman, Okla., 1951), pp. 7–8.
9. *Poetry* (Chicago) 1 (November, 1912), 65.
10. Glenn Hughes, *Imagism and the Imagists: A Study in Modern Poetry* (Stanford, 1931), pp. 30–31. See also Coffman, pp. 14–17.
11. Coffman, pp. 29–30.
12. Hughes, p. 44.
13. Ibid., pp. 41–42. See also Coffman, pp. 30–31.
14. Anon., "Life in a Hothouse," *Newsweek*, May 2, 1960, pp. 196–97.
15. Henry Williamson in *Richard Aldington: An Intimate Portrait*, p. 165.
16. Ibid., p. 121.
17. Ibid., pp. 21–22.
18. Hughes, p. 10.
19. Letter from Richard Aldington to Harry T. Moore, in *Richard Aldington: An Intimate Portrait*, p. 91. See also Randall, ibid., pp. 117–18.
20. Ibid. See also Frank MacShane, *The Life and Work of Ford Madox Ford* (New York, 1965), p. 127.
21. Notice in *The Egoist* 3 (June 1, 1916), 85.
22. *Richard Aldington: An Intimate Portrait*, p. vii.
23. H. D. (Hilda Doolittle), *Bid Me to Live* (New York, 1960), p. 11.

181

24. Ibid., pp. 24–25. See also Vincent Quinn, *Hilda Doolittle (H. D.)* (New York, 1967), p. 27.

25. Ibid., p. 47.

26. *D. H. Lawrence: A Composite Biography*, ed. Edward Nehls, 3 volumes (Madison, Wisc., 1957–1959), III, 595. See also Quinn, pp. 26–27; H. D., pp. 69–70; Harry T. Moore, *The Intelligent Heart: The Story of D. H. Lawrence* (New York, 1962), pp. 298–300.

27. H. D., pp. 47–49, 116–17, 128–30.

28. Quinn, p. 28.

29. *Richard Aldington: An Intimate Portrait*, p. 119. See also *D. H. Lawrence: A Composite Biography*, III, 70, 113, 241, 251–52, 254–55.

30. Quinn, pp. 27–28.

31. *D. H. Lawrence: A Composite Biography*, I, 507.

32. Ibid., III, 69–70.

33. Ibid., pp. 113–14.

34. Ibid., p. 252.

35. Ibid., pp. 265–67.

36. Derek Patmore, ed., *My Friends When Young: The Memoirs of Brigit Patmore* (London, 1968), pp. 1, 3, 102.

37. Ibid., pp. 8, 11, 60, 62, 66–69, 72–73, 80–81, 93–94, 102.

38. *D. H. Lawrence: A Composite Biography*, III, 252, 254–61, 266–67.

39. *My Friends When Young: The Memoirs of Brigit Patmore*, pp. 1, 2, 43, 81, 95. See also John Cournos, *Autobiography* (New York, 1935), illustration facing p. 288.

40. Ibid., pp. 38, 148–49.

41. Ibid., p. 41.

42. Ibid., pp. 41–42.

43. Miriam J. Benkovitz, "Nine for Reeves: Letters from Richard Aldington," *Bulletin of the New York Public Library* 69 (1965), 370, n. 131.

44. *Richard Aldington: An Intimate Portrait*, p. viii.

45. Ibid., pp. viii, 106–108, 130.

46. Ibid., p. 131.

47. Ibid., pp. 15, 27.

48. Ibid., pp. viii, 15–16, 28, 109, 167–68.

49. Ibid., p. 33. See also pp. viii, 16.

50. Ibid., p. 41. See also pp. xv, 45.

51. *Richard Aldington: Selected Critical Writings, 1928–1960*, ed. Alister Kershaw (Carbondale, Ill., 1970), pp. vii–x, xviii–xx. See also *Richard Aldington: An Intimate Portrait*, pp. viii, 16, 20, 22–23, 34, 40–41, 44–46, 48, 61–62, 80, 86–88, 93–94, 120, 143, 154–56, 168.

52. *Richard Aldington: An Intimate Portrait*, pp. 95–96, 143–44.

53. Ibid., pp. xv, 94.

54. Ibid., pp. 46–48. See also pp. viii, xv, 22, 34, 87–89, 101–102, 118–19, 131, 142, 144.

55. Ibid., pp. 34–36.
56. Ibid., pp. 80–81.
57. Ibid., pp. 120–21.
58. Ibid., pp. 78–79.
59. Ibid., p. 62.
60. Ibid., pp. 20–21.
61. Ibid., p. 143.
62. Ibid., p. 46. See also p. 163.
63. Ibid., p. 22. See also pp. 50, 62, 78, 144.
64. Ibid., p. 121. See also pp. 62, 96, 144.
65. Ibid., pp. viii, 17–18, 39, 48–50, 105, 121, 144, 157–61, 171–74.
66. Ibid., pp. viii, 50–51.

Chapter Two

1. Hughes, p. vii.
2. Ibid., pp. 9–10. See also F. S. Flint, "The History of Imagism," *The Egoist* 2 (May, 1915), 70.
3. Ibid, p. 11. See also Flint, 70.
4. Flint, 71. See also Hughes, p. 11.
5. Hughes, p. 12. See also Flint, 71.
6. Ibid., p. 18.
7. *The Complete Poems of Richard Aldington* (London, 1948), p. 13.
8. Hughes, p. 33.
9. Ibid., p. 39.
10. Amy Lowell, ed., *Some Imagist Poets: An Anthology* (Boston, 1915), pp. vi–vii.
11. References to Aldington's *The Complete Poems of Richard Aldington* are hereafter cited in text as *CP*.
12. Hughes, pp. 88–89.
13. *CP*, p. 16.
14. Ibid.
15. Hughes, p. 89.
16. Thomas McGreevy, *Richard Aldington: An Englishman* (London, 1931), p. 15.
17. Ibid., p. 16.
18. Coffman, pp. 97–98.
19. The *Encyclopaedia Britannica* (1972) indicates that the asphodel's "general connection with death is due no doubt to the grayish colour of its leaves and its yellowish flowers, which suggest the gloom of the underworld and the pallor of death."
20. Coffman, pp. 165–66.
21. Ibid., p. 98.
22. Ibid.

23. *The Love of Myrrhine and Konallis, and Other Prose Poems* (Cleveland, 1917).

24. Hughes, p. 96.

25. References to the 1926 (Chicago) edition of *Myrrhine and Konallis* are cited as *MK*.

26. May Sinclair, "The Poems of Richard Aldington," *The English Review* (London) 32 (May, 1921), 403.

27. Ibid.

28. Ibid.

29. Ibid., 400–401.

30. Hughes, p. 55.

31. See "Living Sepulchres," in *The Complete Poems of Richard Aldington*, p. 86.

32. Hughes, p. 55.

33. Coffman, pp. 166–67. See Ezra Pound, "A Few Don'ts by an Imagiste," *Poetry* (Chicago) 1 (March, 1913), 200.

34. Harold G. Henderson, *An Introduction to Haiku: An Anthology of Poems and Poets from Bashō to Shiki* (Garden City, N.Y., 1958), pp. 18–19.

35. Ibid., p. 2.

36. Richard Eugene Smith, "Ezra Pound and the Haiku," *College English* 26 (April, 1965), 523–25.

37. Coffman, p. 167.

38. Henderson, pp. 18–19.

39. Earl Miner, *The Japanese Tradition in British and American Literature* (Princeton, 1958), p. 115. See also Donald Keene, *Japanese Literature: An Introduction for Western Readers* (New York, 1955), pp. 39–41.

40. Translated by Donald Keene in *Anthology of Japanese Literature: From the Earliest Era to the Mid-Nineteenth Century* (New York, 1955), p. 77.

41. Keene, *Japanese Literature: An Introduction for Western Readers*, p. 37. See pp. 31–46 for a survey of the Japanese linked-verse tradition.

42. Coffman, p. 165.

43. This line, '*Mon semblable, mon frère!*', is a quotation of the last line of the opening poem in Baudelaire's *Fleurs du Mal* (1857). It is also quoted in line 76 of T. S. Eliot's *The Waste Land* (1922). Aldington's use of the phrase is apparently earlier than Eliot's; "Interlude" is included among his earliest verse in *The Complete Poems*.

Chapter Three

1. McGreevy, pp. 26–27. See also p. 18.

2. *Images of War* (London, 1919), *Images of Desire* (London, 1919), and *Exile and Other Poems* (London, 1923) have been republished in *The Com-*

plete Poems of Richard Aldington. All quotations are from *The Complete Poems*.

3. *Life for Life's Sake*, pp. 119–20.

4. *The Complete Poems*, p. 302.

5. McGreevy, pp. 28–29.

6. See Hughes, p. 95.

7. C. P. Snow in *Richard Aldington: An Intimate Portrait*, p. 140. See also p. 11, where Roy Campbell makes a similar remark: Aldington "has written some of the finest love poetry of our time."

8. Hughes, p. 95.

9. Ibid., p. 97.

10. *Life for Life's Sake*, p. 207.

11. Ibid., p. 215.

12. McGreevy, p. 26.

Chapter Four

1. Quoted by Hughes, pp. 100–101, from Humbert Wolfe, *Dialogues and Monologues* (New York, 1928); no page reference given.

2. McGreevy, p. 41.

3. C. P. Snow, *Richard Aldington: An Appreciation* (London, n.d.), p. 18.

4. Hughes, p. 101.

5. T. S. Eliot, *The Waste Land* (1922), note on line 218.

6. Dilyara Zhantieva in *Richard Aldington: An Intimate Portrait*, p. 170.

7. McGreevy, p. 42.

8. Ibid.

9. Ibid., p. 43.

10. Hughes, p. 101.

11. McGreevy, p. 43.

12. D. H. Lawrence, "Benjamin Franklin," in *Studies in Classic American Literature* (New York, 1923), p. 10.

13. Line 128. See Bruce R. McElderry, Jr., "Eliot's 'Shakespeherian Rag'," *American Quarterly* 9 (1957), 185–86.

14. Hughes, p. 103.

15. *Life for Life's Sake*, p. 332.

16. Ibid., pp. 62–63.

17. Derek Patmore, ed., *My Friends When Young: The Memoirs of Brigit Patmore*, pp. 22–23, 104.

18. *Life for Life's Sake*, p. 321.

19. See Barbara Smythe, *Trobador Poets: Selections from the Poems of Eight Trobadors: Translated from the Provençal with Introductions and Notes* (London, 1929), pp. 169–81. See also John Frederick Rowbotham, *The Troubadours and Courts of Love* (London, 1895), pp. 263–69.

20. Snow, pp. 1–2; reprinted in *Richard Aldington: An Intimate Portrait*, p. 134.

21. Ibid., pp. 2–3; reprinted in *Richard Aldington: An Intimate Portrait*, pp. 134–36.

22. Ibid., p. 18.

23. Ibid., p. 5.

24. Ibid., p. 15; reprinted in *Richard Aldington: An Intimate Portrait*, p. 140.

25. Ibid., pp. 19–20.

Chapter Five

1. *Life for Life's Sake*, p. 332. References to *Death of a Hero* (London: Sphere Books, 1969) are hereafter cited in text as *DH*. A recent edition of the book was used because *Death of a Hero* was first published in a somewhat expurgated form.

2. Ibid.

3. See Erich Maria Remarque, *All Quiet on the Western Front*, trans. A. W. Wheen (New York, 1929), pp. 279–80. On rare occasions, certain passages in *Death of a Hero* bear some resemblance to those in Remarque's novel. In a letter to Herbert Read (July 15, 1929), however, Aldington denies having read Remarque's novel "until my own book was in type" (*Richard Aldington: An Intimate Portrait*, p. 129).

4. See *Life for Life's Sake*, p. 346.

5. Ibid., p. 42.

6. Snow, p. 7.

7. See *Life for Life's Sake*, pp. 217–21, 256. See also Aldington's lampoon of T. S. Eliot, "Stepping Heavenward," in *Soft Answers*.

8. See *Life for Life's Sake*, pp. 141, 303–306, 329–34.

9. Ibid., pp. 149–59.

10. Ibid.

11. Ibid., pp. 104–11, 133–40, 216–17, 336.

12. See Cournos, p. 187, for a description of Dorothy Yorke. See also *D. H. Lawrence: A Composite Biography*, III, 70.

13. See William Carlos Williams, *The Autobiography of William Carlos Williams* (New York, 1948), pp. 67–68, for a description of H. D. (Hilda Doolittle).

14. Snow, p. 3; reprinted in *Richard Aldington: An Intimate Portrait*, p. 136.

15. Ibid., p. 6.

16. Ibid., p. 7.

17. *Life for Life's Sake*, pp. 170–72.

18. Ibid., p. 178.

19. Remarque, p. 299.

20. McGreevy, p. 64.

21. Snow, p. 13.

22. *Roads to Glory* (Garden City, N.Y., 1930), p. 205

23. *Life for Life's Sake*, p. 339.

24. Ibid., p. 178.

Chapter Six

1. *Life for Life's Sake*, p. 243. References to *The Colonel's Daughter* (London, 1931) are hereafter cited in text as *CD*.

2. *Life for Life's Sake*, pp. 253–53.

3. *Death of a Hero*, pp. 221–23.

4. *Life for Life's Sake*, p. 332.

5. *Death of a Hero*, p. 18.

6. McGreevy, p. 70.

7. Ibid., p. 71.

8. *Soft Answers*, with a preface by Harry T. Moore (Carbondale, Ill., 1967), p. ix; hereafter cited in text as *SA*.

9. Ibid., pp. xi–xii.

10. Ibid., p. ix.

11. *Life for Life's Sake*, p. 208.

12. *Soft Answers*, p. ix.

13. Murray Schafer, "Ezra Pound and Music," *Ezra Pound: A Collection of Critical Essays*. ed. Walter Sutton (Englewood Cliffs, N.J., 1963), p. 129.

14. Charles Norman, *Ezra Pound* (New York, 1960), pp. 254, 260, 280–82. See also Schafer, pp. 130–34; and *Life for Life's Sake*, p. 70.

15. Ibid., p. 271.

16. Ibid., p. 281.

17. *Life for Life's Sake*, p. 133.

18. Norman, pp. 143–45. See also illustration facing p. 47.

19. *Soft Answers*, p. x.

20. *Richard Aldington: An Intimate Portrait*, pp. 24–25. See also *Soft Answers*, p. xi.

21. *Life for Life's Sake*, p. 256.

22. Hughes, pp. 72–77.

23. *Life for Life's Sake*, p. 133.

24. Ibid., p. 269.

25. *Soft Answers*, p. x.

26. *Life for Life's Sake*, pp. 152–54.

27. Ibid., p. 217.

28. Ibid., pp. 219, 268–69. See also *Soft Answers*, p. x.

29. Snow, pp. 5, 11, 18. References to *All Men Are Enemies: A Romance* (Garden City, N.Y., 1933) are hereafter cited in text as *AM*.

30. Ibid., p. 11.

31. Ibid., p. 5.

32. McGreevy, p. 53.

33. From the long poem *Life Quest* in *The Complete Poems of Richard Aldington*, p. 325.

34. *Life for Life's Sake*, p. 332.

35. I have not checked the Russian editions of the novel to determine if the quoted passages have been altered or omitted by the translators.

36. *Richard Aldington: An Intimate Portrait*, p. 157.

37. Ibid., pp. 152–53.

38. Ibid., pp. 173–74.

39. Derek Patmore, ed., *My Friends When Young: The Memoirs of Brigit Patmore*, pp. 147–48. See also *Life for Life's Sake*, pp. 373–84.

Chapter Seven

1. *Women Must Work: A Novel* (London, 1934) hereafter cited in text as *W*.

2. Snow, p. 11.

3. *Very Heaven* (Garden City, New York, 1937); hereafter cited in text as *VH*.

4. Snow, p. 12.

5. *Seven Against Reeves: A Comedy-Farce* (Garden City, N.Y., 1938); hereafter cited in text as *SR*.

6. Snow, p. 13.

7. *Rejected Guest* (New York, 1939); hereafter cited in text as *RG*.

8. *Life for Life's Sake*, pp. 5–6.

9. *The Romance of Casanova: A Novel* (New York, 1946); hereafter cited in text as *R*.

Chapter Eight

1. *Life for Life's Sake*, pp. 5–6.

2. *Voltaire* (London, 1929), pp. 7–8.

3. Ibid., p. 8.

4. Ibid., p. 138.

5. Ibid., pp. 173–74.

6. Ibid., p. 237.

7. *The Duke: Being an Account of the Life & Achievements of Arthur Wellesley, 1st Duke of Wellington* (New York, 1943), p. 21.

8. *Four English Portraits, 1801–1851* (London, 1948), p. v.

9. Ibid., pp. vi–vii.

10. *The Strange Life of Charles Waterton, 1782–1865* (New York, 1949), p. 9.

11. *D. H. Lawrence: Portrait of a Genius But . . .* (New York, 1950), p. ix.

12. Ibid., p. x.

13. *Pinorman: Personal Recollections of Norman Douglas, Pino Orioli and Charles Prentice* (London, 1954), p. 1.

14. Ibid., p. 28. See also *Life for Life's Sake*, p. 370.

15. *Lawrence of Arabia: A Biographical Enquiry* (Chicago, 1955), p. 11.

16. Henry Williamson in *Richard Aldington: An Intimate Portrait*, p. 168.

17. *Lawrence of Arabia*, p. 14.

18. Ibid., p. 13.

19. Ibid.

20. Ibid., pp. 107–109, 291.

21. Ibid., pp. 26–27.

22. Kershaw, ed., *Richard Aldington: Selected Critical Writings, 1928–1960*, pp. vii–x, xviii–xx. See also *Richard Aldington: An Intimate Portrait*, pp. viii, 16, 20, 22–23, 34, 41–42, 44–46, 51, 61–62, 80, 86–88, 93–94, 120, 143, 154–56, 168.

23. *Richard Aldington: An Intimate Portrait*, p. 96.

24. *Medallions in Clay* (New York, 1921), p. 9.

25. McGreevy, p. 69.

26. Review by "G.R." in *Commonweal* 43 (February 8, 1946), 436.

27. *Life for Life's Sake*, pp. 267–68.

28. Kershaw, ed., *Richard Aldington: Selected Critical Writings, 1928–1960*, p. xv.

29. *Life for Life's Sake*, p. 51.

30. Ibid., p. 240.

31. *Literary Studies and Reviews* (Freeport, N.Y. 1968; reprinted from *Literary Studies and Reviews* (London: George Allen and Unwin, 1924), hereafter cited in text as *LS*.

32. Kershaw, ed., *Richard Aldington: Selected Critical Writings, 1928–1960*, p. xix. See also *Life for Life's Sake*, p. 219.

33. Ibid., pp. 3–4, 7–8.

34. *Life for Life's Sake*, p. 175.

35. Ibid., p. 173.

36. D. Mossop, "Un Disciple de Gourmont: Richard Aldington," *Revue de Littérature Comparée* 25 (October–December, 1951), 403–35.

37. *French Studies and Reviews* (Freeport, N.Y., 1967), p. 209; reprinted from *French Studies and Reviews* (London: George Allen and Unwin, 1926).

38. Kershaw, ed., *Richard Aldington: Selected Critical Writings, 1928–1960*; hereafter cited in text as *RA*.

39. *Artifex: Sketches and Ideas* (Garden City, N.Y., 1936); hereafter cited in text as *A*.

Selected Bibliography

BIBLIOGRAPHY

KERSHAW, ALISTER. *A Bibliography of the Works of Richard Aldington from 1915 to 1948*. Introduction by Richard Aldington. Burlingame, Calif.: William P. Wredon, 1950; London: Quadrant Press, 1950. Complete list of English and American editions, as well as translations into other languages, of Aldington's books which were published up to 1948.

———, and TEMPLE, FRÉDÉRIC-JACQUES. eds. *Richard Aldington: An Intimate Portrait*. Carbondale, Ill.: Southern Illinois University Press, 1965. Collection of twenty-two pieces written by Aldington's friends about his life and work. Contains "A Chronological Check List of the Books by Richard Aldington" (pp. 175–86) prepared by Paul Schlueter.

PRIMARY SOURCES

1. Books
Since the majority of books were published concurrently in England and America, preference is given to American editions unless they were issued later than the English editions. Recent reprints are also listed.

Images (1910–1915). London: Poetry Bookshop, 1915.
The Love of Myrrhine and Konallis, and Other Prose Poems. Cleveland: Clerk's Press, 1917.
Images of War: A Book of Poems. London: George Allen and Unwin, 1919.
Images of Desire. London: Elkin Mathews, 1919.
Exile and Other Poems. London: George Allen and Unwin, 1923.
A Fool i' the Forest: A Phantasmagoria. London: George Allen and Unwin, 1924.
Literary Studies and Reviews. London: George Allen and Unwin, 1924; Freeport, N.Y.: Books for Libraries Press, 1968.
Voltaire. New York: E. P. Dutton, 1925.
French Studies and Reviews. New York: Dial Press, 1926; Freeport, N.Y.: Books for Libraries Press, 1967.

The Eaten Heart. Chapelle-Reanville, Eure, France: Hours Press, 1929.

Death of a Hero: A Novel. New York: Covici, Friede, 1929; London: Sphere Books (unexpurgated edition), 1969.

Roads to Glory. Garden City, N.Y.: Doubleday, Doran, 1930.

A Dream in the Luxembourg. London: Chatto and Windus, 1930.

Imagist Anthology, 1930. New York: Covici, Friede, 1930.

The Colonel's Daughter: A Novel. Garden City, N.Y.: Doubleday, Doran, 1931.

Soft Answers. Garden City, N.Y.: Doubleday, Doran, 1932; Carbondale: Southern Illinois University Press, 1967.

All Men Are Enemies: A Romance. Garden City, N.Y.: Doubleday, Doran, 1933.

Women Must Work: A Novel. Garden City, N.Y.: Doubleday, Doran, 1934.

Life Quest. Garden City, N.Y.: Doubleday, Doran, 1935.

Artifex: Sketches and Ideas. London: Chatto and Windus, 1935; Garden City, N.Y.: Doubleday, Doran, 1936.

The Crystal World. London: William Heinemann, 1937.

Very Heaven. Garden City, N.Y.: Doubleday, Doran, 1937.

Seven Against Reeves: A Comedy-Farce. Garden City, N.Y.: Doubleday, Doran, 1938.

Rejected Guest: A Novel. New York: Viking Press, 1939.

Life for Life's Sake: A Book of Reminiscences. New York: Viking Press, 1941; London: Cassell, 1968.

The Viking Book of Poetry of the English-Speaking World. New York: Viking Press, 1941.

The Duke: Being an Account of the Life & Achievements of Arthur Wellesley, 1st Duke of Wellington. New York: Viking Press, 1943.

The Romance of Casanova: A Novel. New York: Duell, Sloan, and Pearce, 1946.

The Complete Poems of Richard Aldington. London: Allan Wingate, 1948.

Four English Portraits, 1801–1851. London: Evans Brothers, 1948.

The Strange Life of Charles Waterton, 1782–1865. New York: Duell, Sloan, and Pearce, 1949.

D. H. Lawrence: Portrait of a Genius But . . . New York: Duell, Sloan, and Pearce, 1950.

The Religion of Beauty: Selections from the Aesthetes. London: William Heinemann, 1950.

Pinorman: Personal Recollections of Norman Douglas, Pino Orioli and Charles Prentice. London: William Heinemann, 1954.

Lawrence of Arabia: A Biographical Enquiry. Chicago: Henry Regnery, 1955.

Introduction to Mistral. London: William Heinemann, 1956; Carbondale: Southern Illinois University Press, 1960.

Frauds. London: William Heinemann, 1957.

Portrait of a Rebel: The Life and Works of Robert Louis Stevenson. London: Evans Brothers, 1957.

Richard Aldington: Selected Critical Writings, 1928–1960. Edited by Alister Kershaw. Carbondale: Southern Illinois University Press, 1970.

2. Translations

Medallions in Clay. New York: Alfred A. Knopf, 1921.

French Comedies of the XVIIIth Century. New York: E. P. Dutton, [1923]. *The Residuary Legatee,* by Regnard; *Turcaret, or the Financier,* by Lesage; *The Game of Love and Chance,* by Marivaux; *The Conceited Count,* by Destouches.

Voyages to the Moon and the Sun, by Cyrano de Bergerac. New York: E. P. Dutton, [1923].

Dangerous Acquaintances (Les Liaisons Dangereuses), by Choderlos de Laclos. New York: E. P. Dutton, [1924]. Reprinted in 1946 in *Great French Romances* by Duell, Sloan, and Pearce, New York.

Sturly, by Pierre Custot. Boston: Houghton Mifflin, 1924.

A Book of 'Characters' from Theophrastus; Joseph Hall, Sir Thomas Overbury, Nicolas Breton, John Earle, Thomas Fuller, and Other English Authors; Jean De La Bruyère, Vauvenargues, and Other French Authors. New York: E. P. Dutton, [1924].

The Fifteen Joys of Marriage. New York: E. P. Dutton, [1926]. Ascribed to Antoine De La Sale, ca. 1388–1462.

Candide and Other Romances, by Voltaire. New York: E. P. Dutton, [1927]. *Candide* reprinted in 1959 by Hanover House, Garden City, N.Y.

Letters of Madame de Sévigné to Her Daughter and Her Friends. London: George Routledge, 1927.

Letters of Voltaire and Frederick the Great. New York: Brentano's, 1927.

Letters of Voltaire and Madame du Deffand. New York: Brentano's, 1927.

The Treason of the Intellectuals (La Trahison des Clercs), by Julien Benda. New York: William Morrow, 1928.

Fifty Romance Lyric Poems. New York: Crosby Gaige, 1928; London: Chatto and Windus, 1931.

Remy de Gourmont: Selections from All His Works. 2 vols. New York: Covici, Friede, 1929.

The Decameron of Giovanni Boccaccio. New York: Covici, Friede, 1930; Garden City, N.Y.: Doubleday, 1949.

A Wreath for San Gemignano. New York: Duell, Sloan, and Pearce, 1945.

SECONDARY SOURCES

BAUM, PAULL F. "Mr. Richard Aldington." *South Atlantic Quarterly* 28 (April, 1929), 201–208. Scholarly criticism of Aldington's poetry.

BENKOVITZ, MIRIAM J., ed. *A Passionate Prodigality: Letters to Alan Bird from Richard Aldington, 1949–1962.* New York: New York Public Library/Readex Books, 1976. Annotated edition of the letters, with a biographical glossary and an index.

————, ed. "Nine for Reeves: Letters from Richard Aldington." *Bulletin of the New York Public Library* 69 (1965), 349–74. Nine letters written by Aldington between 1930 and 1933 to a young admirer. For the most part, the letters discuss literary matters. Notes by the editor are also very useful.

COFFMAN, STANLEY K., JR. *Imagism: A Chapter for the History of Modern Poetry.* Norman, Okla.: University of Oklahoma Press, 1951. Discussion of the history, principles, and influence of the imagist movement. Also contains valuable criticism of Aldington's early poems.

COURNOS, JOHN. *Autobiography.* New York: Putnam's, 1935. Since Cournos was one of Aldington's closest friends until the end of World War I, the book tells much about Aldington and some of the important people in his life.

DOOLITTLE, HILDA (H. D.). *Bid Me to Live.* New York: Grove Press, 1960. An autobiographical novel by Aldington's first wife; gives a fictionalized account of their marriage and its subsequent dissolution. Rafe and Julia Ashton may be identified as Richard and Hilda Aldington; Bella, as Dorothy "Arabella" Yorke.

FLINT, F. S. "The History of Imagism." *The Egoist* 2 (May, 1915), 70–71. Account of the origins and history (to 1914) of the imagist movement by one of the major imagists.

GALLOWAY, RUTH E. "The Poetry of Richard Aldington: A Critical Introduction." Ph.D. dissertation, Texas Tech University, 1972. Assessment of Aldington's poetic achievement.

GATES, NORMAN T. "Richard Aldington's Personal Notes on Poetry." *Texas Quarterly* 17 (Spring, 1974), 107–13. Aldington's poetic principles expressed in a previously unpublished notebook which he probably wrote during the 1920s.

————. *The Poetry of Richard Aldington: A Critical Evaluation and an Anthology of Uncollected Poems.* University Park, Penn.: Pennsylvania State University Press, 1974. The first part of this book deals with a review of criticism of Aldington's poetry, a survey of editions published before *The Complete Poems*, an evaluation of Aldington's poetic achievement, and a commentary on *The Complete Poems*. The second part contains 216 poems which were not included in *The Complete Poems*. The book also contains a valuable bibliography of primary and secondary sources.

————, *A Checklist of the Letters of Richard Aldington.* Carbondale, Ill.: Southern Illinois University Press, 1977. The most recent and most complete list of letters written by Aldington.

HUGHES, GLENN. *Imagism and the Imagists: A Study in Modern Poetry.* Stanford, Calif.: Stanford University Press, 1931. Reprint. N.Y.:

Humanities Press, 1960. Deals with the origins and development of imagism, the controversies, the responses of the critics, and the poems of the major imagists. Chapter 5, "Richard Aldington: The Rebel," includes criticism of some of Aldington's later poems, as well as of his earlier imagist verse.

KEENE, DONALD. *Japanese Literature: An Introduction for Western Readers.* New York: Grove Press, 1955. Comments on the influence of Japanese short verse on the poetry of some of the leading imagists, including Aldington.

KITTREDGE, SELWYN BURNETT. "The Literary Career of Richard Aldington." Ph.D. dissertation, New York University, 1976. Discussion of Aldington's writings in terms of themes and literary movements.

KNIGHTLEY, PHILLIP. "Aldington's Enquiry Concerning T. E. Lawrence." *Texas Quarterly* 16 (Winter, 1973), 98–105. Brief account of the conspiracy to prevent the publication of Aldington's biography of Lawrence of Arabia.

LOWELL, AMY, ed. *Some Imagist Poets.* 3 vols. Boston: Houghton Mifflin, 1915, 1916, 1917. Three of the five official anthologies of imagist verse; each contains different poems by the same six major imagists, including Aldington.

MCGREEVY, THOMAS. *Richard Aldington: An Englishman.* London: Chatto and Windus, 1931. Until my book, McGreevy's has been the only published book-length study (73 pages) in English of both the prose and poetry of Richard Aldington. It contains appreciative criticism of Aldington's works up to the year 1931.

MOSSOP, D. "Un Disciple de Gourmont: Richard Aldington." *Revue de Littérature Comparée* 25 (October–December, 1951), 403–35. French study of the influence of Remy de Gourmont on Aldington's writings.

NEHLS, EDWARD, ed. *D. H. Lawrence: A Composite Biography.* 3 vols. Madison, Wisc.: University of Wisconsin Press, 1957–1959. Contains biographical information about Aldington and three of the most important women in his life: Hilda Doolittle (H. D.), Dorothy "Arabella" Yorke, and Brigit Patmore.

PATMORE, BRIGIT. *My Friends When Young: The Memoirs of Brigit Patmore.* Edited with an introduction by Derek Patmore. London: William Heinemann, 1968. Aldington had a love affair with Brigit Patmore which lasted for about ten years. Both the *Memoirs* and the introduction by her son, Derek, provide much information about her life with Aldington.

POUND, EZRA, ed. *Des Imagistes: An Anthology.* New York: Albert and Charles Boni, 1914. First official collection of imagist poetry. Aldington contributed the largest number of poems to this volume.

QUINN, VINCENT. *Hilda Doolittle (H. D.).* New York: Twayne Publishers, 1967. Study of the life and writings of Aldington's first wife; provides information about his relationship with her.

ROSENTHAL, SIDNEY. "The Fiction of Richard Aldington." Ph. D. dissertation, Harvard University, 1968. A study of Aldington's achievement in prose fiction.

SINCLAIR, MAY. "The Poems of Richard Aldington." *The English Review* (London) 32 (May, 1921), 397–410. Appreciative evaluation of Aldington's early poems and translations.

SNOW, CHARLES PERCY. *Richard Aldington: An Appreciation.* London: William Heinemann, n. d. [1938?]. Pamphlet (26 pages) by the well-known novelist and critic. Contains highly appreciative criticism of Aldington's works up to the year 1938, plus a bibliography.

THATCHER, DAVID S., ed. "Richard Aldington's Letters to Herbert Read." *Malahat Review*, no. 15 (1970), 5–44. Aldington's correspondence with a friend and fellow writer whom he had known since World War I.

URNOV, MIKHAIL V. *Ričard Oldington.* Moscow: Vysšaja škola, 1968. Study of Aldington by a Soviet scholar. Soviet critics regard Aldington as one of the most important English writers of the twentieth century.

Work in progress: Biographies of Richard Aldington by Charles D. Doyle (University of Victoria) and Harry T. Moore (Southern Illinois University). An edition of Aldington's letters and a book on the Aldington-Lawrence Durrell correspondence by Harry T. Moore. A new Aldington bibliography by Ann Bagnell (Temple University) and Stephen Jay Pike (Temple University Press). A study of Russian criticism of Aldington's writings by Norman T. Gates (Rider College) and Robert J. Winter (Rider College).

Index

(The works of Aldington are listed under his name)